THE CHURCH'S BIBLE

THE CHURCH'S BIBLE

Its Contemporary Authority

Darrell Jodock

Fortress Press   Minneapolis

THE CHURCH'S BIBLE
Its Contemporary Authority

Cover Design: Dawn Mathers
Internal Design: Carol Evans-Smith

Library of Congress Cataloging-in-Publication Data

Jodock, Darrell, 1941-
    The church's Bible: its contemporary authority / Darrell Jodock.
        p. cm.
    Bibliography: p.   B5
    Includes index.   480
    ISBN 0-8006-2326-6
    1. Bible—Evidences, authority, etc.   I. Title.   .J56
    BS480.J56   1989   88-45827
    220.1'3—dc20   1989   CIP

Manufactured in the U.S.A.   AF 1-2326

93   92   91   90   89   1   2   3   4   5   6   7   8   9   10

To JJ,
in gratitude for her love

Contents

Preface   ix

Introduction   1

PART ONE   The Modern Challenge to Biblical Authority

  1. Authority as Problematic in the Modern Era   15
  2. Responses within a Static World View   31
  3. Responses within a Dynamic World View   51

PART TWO   Toward a Contemporary View

  4. The Bible in Postmodern Culture   71
  5. God's Presence, Revelation, and Inspiration   89
  6. Biblical Usefulness, Biblical Authority   105
  7. Recontextualizing the Bible   129

Epilogue   145

Notes   147

For Further Reading   159

Index   169

Preface

The Bible is an important asset for the community of believers, but often its voice is obscured by conflicting interpretations. Does it support equality for women or does it endorse paternalism? Does the Bible condemn all homosexuality or only sexual exploitation whether practiced by homosexuals or heterosexuals? Does it endorse the American dream or prophetically expose the shortcomings of Western society? Voices claiming the Bible as their authority advocate widely differing views.

When exposed to such conflict, persons seeking religious and moral insight often despair. Everything seems to hinge on the approach to the text. Who is to decide, they wonder, whether the liberals or the conservatives offer the better interpretation?

I believe we need a contemporary theory of biblical authority that can move the discussion beyond the seemingly endless conflict between rival patterns of interpretation. The interpretive procedure it outlines must focus discussion rather than close it off. It must make the Bible available for addressing contemporary ethical, religious, and societal issues rather than imprison it within the walls of unproductive conflict and constricted perspective.

To construct such a theory, we must assess the past in order to understand the dynamics underlying existing approaches to the Bible and we must assess the present in order to locate the societal features that need to be taken into account today. We must identify clearly the components of a contemporary theory and also show how an integrated view can be constructed. Such is the task of this book.

The book's preparation began in 1976, when David L. Tiede and I were on the faculty of Luther (now Luther Northwestern) Theological Seminary in St. Paul, Minnesota. During our interviews with seminary seniors we were struck by the ease with which they voiced objections to the theories of biblical authority they found unacceptable and by the difficulty they had in explaining a positive approach of their own.

One reason for this occurred to us: the subject was inherently interdisciplinary and fell "between the cracks" of the various departments of a theological seminary. We therefore proposed a team-taught, interdisciplinary course in the authority of the Bible. David would represent biblical studies and I historical theology. A grant from the Aid Association for Lutherans provided us with released time to prepare the course, which we entitled "The Church's Bible and the Gospel Truth."

We taught it twice before I left in 1978 to join the faculty of Muhlenberg College, in Allentown, Pennsylvania.

Preparing for the course and teaching it were both immensely rewarding experiences. David and I discovered new perspectives and noticed connections we had never seen before. Our excitement led us to discuss the possibility of a book, quite different from this one, in which he and I wrote alternating chapters. When I moved to another part of the country, David encouraged me to pursue a writing project on my own. The present volume is the result. I extend my thanks to him for the stimulation of our work together and for his ongoing encouragement, including his comments on the initial draft of this book.

Thanks are also due to the Aid Association for Lutherans for their financial support, to the seminary administration for approving released time, and to our students for their enthusiastic and thoughtful involvement in the issues of the course.

The actual preparation of the book began in 1982-83, while I was a resident fellow at the Institute for Ecumenical and Cultural Research, in Collegeville, Minnesota. In that hospitable setting, amid the marvelous companionship of several other scholars, an initial draft took shape. My colleagues there represented at least five denominations other than my own; our stimulating discussions made the benefits of an ecumenical perspective very apparent. Our social life and shared worship life, both of which developed quickly and easily, were also vivid reminders of the breadth and importance of the community of faith. To the Institute, to my colleagues there, to Robert Bilheimer, its (now retired) director, to Sister Dolores Schuh and Brother Wilfrid, and to many others at St. John's, I express my thanks.

My experience at the Ecumenical Institute was possible only because Muhlenberg College granted a sabbatical leave, for which I am most grateful. I also received summer study grants in 1984 and 1986. Colleagues at Muhlenberg have been an unfailing source of encouragement. I have benefited from the valuable comments of Professors Rodney Ring, Daniel Wilson, and Robert Kysar, each of whom read the manuscript.

Several groups of clergy and laity have heard me explore in differing ways the issues addressed in the book. I have benefited greatly from their comments and criticisms. Especially noteworthy are clergy in two seminars I taught in the graduate program of the Lutheran Theological Seminary at Philadelphia in 1981; clergy and spouses at the 1981 Wartburg Academy of the West, in Thousand Oaks, California; and those at the Genesis event in Stroudsburg, Pennsylvania, in April 1986. I am also grateful to the participants in the 1983 School of Religion in Tamaqua, Pennsylvania; members of my class at the 1985 Lay Academy in Allentown, Pennsylvania; and participants in a Northeastern Pennsylvania Synod workshop for church-school teachers, "How Lutherans View the Bible: Sorting Out Some Contemporary Issues," held in February 1986.

Professional peers in the American Academy of Religion have been helpful, especially members of the Roman Catholic Modernism Group and the Nineteenth Century Theology Working Group with whom I have explored pieces of this project. My thanks to them and to members of the Ecumenical Seminar of the Lehigh Valley Associated Independent Colleges who engaged in a lively session on this topic in September 1984.

I have found give-and-take to be the most valuable way to clarify my own thoughts. Therefore, I extend my gratitude to every conversation partner who has contributed to the development of the thoughts expressed in this book.

I have said that preparation for this book began in 1976, but in a deeper sense it started long before. My parental home shaped my basic attitudes toward authority, and the solid wisdom of my childhood pastor, Dr. Arthur Rholl, influenced in deep and significant ways my fundamental perceptions of the Bible. A great deal has happened since then, but the contributions of my childhood home and church remain an important part of who I am and whatever insight I may have to offer. The same can be said for my teachers at St. Olaf College, Luther Theological Seminary, Union Theological Seminary, and Yale University who opened the doors of the world for me.

For many among us the authority of the Bible remains a troublesome topic, one that surfaces in almost every Bible study and every Christian discussion of controversial contemporary issues. The topic deserves as much clarity as can be brought to it. I hope the present treatise advances that cause.

Darrell Jodock
Muhlenberg College
Allentown, Pennsylvania

Introduction

Epochs of church history may be characterized by the questions that perplex and puzzle church members and occupy their attention. Christology and the Trinity were, for example, major concerns of the fourth and fifth centuries. Throughout the Middle Ages theologians in the West puzzled over divine sovereignty and human freedom, and later in that era they debated vigorously about church authority. The Reformation period concerned itself with questions of salvation: grace, faith, and works. So distinctive were the discussions of the Reformation that its contemporary descendants of the Reformation are often puzzled to discover that the fathers of the second and third centuries could be so casual about soteriological distinctions later deemed crucial.

Church members in each epoch also assume a certain frame of reference or employ a set of axioms that define the boundaries of their discussions. The Trinitarian controversies of the fourth century, for example, assumed particular notions of transcendence, divine nature, and human nature, all of which influenced the course of the argument. Likewise, the debates of the Middle Ages were conducted within an Augustinian framework whose definitions of God and God's relationship to time set limits to the theological options that could be considered.

Two, or possibly three, questions have preoccupied Christians during the past two centuries: questions of authority in the church (whether the authority of the Bible, of dogma, or of the papacy), of the relationship between Christianity and modern society, and (possibly) of ecumenical relations. Of these, the first two are closely related, because since the eighteenth century modern culture's challenge to inherited assumptions about authority in general has required renewed discussions of authority in the church. Not only are the two issues interlocked, they have often come together in a single set of questions regarding the character and authority of the Bible.

Whenever scientific discoveries (such as the so-called natural laws of gravity and motion or the theory of evolution) challenged the validity of Christian claims (e.g., regarding miracles), the authority of the Bible seemed to be at stake. Whenever societal standards (e.g., regarding slavery or sexual conduct) ran counter to Christian sensibilities, the authority of the Bible seemed under attack. Whenever it was believed that society was improving and that this progress could be detected, the question arose whether the Bible was becoming obsolete.

This book will analyze the forces at work in the modern debates about the Bible and its authority. It will seek to describe the tensions between Christianity and modern culture which fueled those debates and to outline several ways in which Christians have endeavored to deal with them. Because any particular understanding of the Bible's authority contains several components, the discussion will seek to uncover the role and status of each. It will also seek to show that any theory of biblical authority is inherently contextual. On the basis of these observations the book will proceed to outline a contemporary, contextually postmodern, and suggestively comprehensive understanding of the character, use, and authority of the Bible.

The first three chapters will analyze the modern debates. The last four chapters will construct a contemporary theory of biblical authority. This "introduction" endeavors to accomplish three purposes: to explain why I propose a coherent and comprehensive understanding of biblical authority, to assess the status and importance of the topic, and to identify some features of the theological and cultural setting in which this discussion occurs.

The Need for a Coherent Theory

This volume is in response to my realization that many, even with theological training, lack a coherent understanding of the role of Scripture in the church. The problem seems to have developed because we are saddled with options now fast becoming obsolete. Though each of these options may once have been a creative response to problems, like well-worn ruts in a road they are now hardened categories, ill suited to the church's engagement with contemporary issues. Persons wrestling with contemporary issues often work with unexamined, inappropriate, and sometimes even contradictory assumptions about the authority of the Bible. They are convinced that the Bible is important but, lacking a coherent explanation of its relevance, have patched together mismatched procedures and biblical interpretations. No wonder the reasons offered for the importance of one passage do not seem to apply to other important sections of the Bible.

More specifically, seminary training may have left clergy without an integrated view of biblical authority. The topic cuts across theological disciplines and thus is addressed only piecemeal by most curricula. Persons may emerge with an understanding of revelation and inspiration, for example, that is at odds with their exegetical practice. Their biblical studies may have habituated them to the discipline of historical-critical study, but they use the discipline without integrating it into any coherent theological outlook. They may be clear about what views of biblical authority they oppose but may be unable to explain one they endorse. Their interpretation of biblical passages may therefore often seem haphazard or puzzling to their listeners, who may as a result either slide back into one of the well-worn ruts or, worse yet, despair of learning anything at all from the Bible.

The lack of a coherent understanding of the role of the Scriptures in the church influences the character and purpose of this book, which seeks to construct an *integrated contemporary* view of the nature and authority of the Bible. If the underlying problem has been correctly diagnosed, then one crucial step will be a careful analysis of what is and is not out-of-date. We must examine the ruts and the reasons why they have been created, and we must diagnose, as best we can, the character of contemporary society in order to set the stage for an integrated understanding of the Bible's authority. Another crucial step will be to identify as clearly as possible the ingredients out of which this contemporary understanding of the authority of the Bible is being built. As appropriate pieces are put together an integrated view will take shape.

Certain risks are inherent in this project. An important one arises from the fact that it will be necessary to make assertions about a wide range of topics, each of which is open to debate, disagreement, and controversy. A fully argued justification at every juncture would be desirable but would also ill suit the main purpose of the volume. Inevitably, many of the claims of the book as they now stand will seem inadequately substantiated and defended, especially to those who find them unusual or objectionable. In particular, the descriptions of modern and postmodern culture are extremely general. They are intended to be suggestive and to illustrate the role played by cultural context in a theory of biblical authority. Amplifications, revisions, and further specifications are needed, but they will not alter the value of an integrated view that pays attention to *some* definition of modern and postmodern culture.

Moreover, the six positions outlined in chapters 2 and 3 are highly schematic. A fuller treatment would require citations for each feature within the composite description and case studies to show how these ideas have influenced interpretations made by their proponents. The theological judgments that influence the course of the constructive argument also deserve far fuller treatment, as do the procedures sketched for the appropriate use of the Bible.

I am convinced that one crucial ingredient in theological thinking is a sense of humor. Important things need to be said, but they are misunderstood if taken too seriously. This is because theological thinking is always in service to life—to a living God, living human beings, and a lived God-human relationship. To take a theological statement too seriously would be to lose sight of that which it seeks to illumine. The reader of this volume is encouraged to approach many of its assertions with an appropriate sense of humor, examining them for what they are worth in relation to the overall purpose of the book—in relation, that is, to constructing an integrated contemporary understanding of the Bible and its authority.

In the light of this purpose, I extend to the reader a twofold invitation: to examine the components presented here (e.g., a view of revelation, an understanding of authority, a perspective on contemporary society) in relation to one another to judge whether they cohere in ways and to a degree not possible if the issues they concern are understood differently; and to consider (if the reader believes any of the components to be inadequate) whether an alternative pattern of contemporary coherence can be envisioned. A valuable purpose will have been served if this book catalyzes theological integration and contemporary theological reflection, even along lines quite different from its own.

A Comprehensive Topic

A theory of biblical authority is like a spider web. To be stable it must be anchored to many other topics. Among them are one's concept of God and of the way God interacts with the world, one's portrayal of history and of historical change and continuity, one's view of the sinful predicament of humanity and of the range of potentialities available to sinful and redeemed human beings, one's view of revelation, one's understanding of the immanence and transcendence of God, and one's estimate of the importance of the church as a human community, the value of the written over against the spoken, and the source and character of religious knowledge. A coherent view cannot be established without examining the lines connecting the question with these and other anchor points. The scope of the task is almost as large as the scope of theology itself: any attempt to sketch a coherent overview of the entire web is bound to remain incomplete. Yet it is better done incompletely than not at all.

My analogy is not meant to suggest, however, that defining a view of scriptural authority is *the* central or *the* foundational question for theology. It is not *the* basis for all theological issues nor even the only place where they all meet. No single theological locus may in fact be that basic or that central. But if some question is *the* central or *the* foundational question of theology, better candidates are available for the honor than the question of the status of the Bible—namely, questions concerning the identity of God or the person and work of Jesus the Christ.

Whatever the candidates for the central spot, however, the issue of biblical authority is closely tied to each of them.

The Importance of the Topic

Scriptural authority is not foundational. As I shall try to show in this book, it is in fact quite derivative. Like a spider web without anchor points, a theory of scriptural authority collapses without an image of revelation, without an image of God, or without a portrait of the community of faith to which it can be tied.

Nor is it necessary that all Christians agree on any one theory of scriptural authority. A group of Christians can profit from the Bible and find its writings religiously useful with or without a "correct" understanding of inspiration or revelation. Some theory—whether worked out or implicit—always guides believers in their approach to the Bible, but more than one theory is possible. Other agreements (e.g., about the character and identity of God and about God's goal for human existence) are more foundational; disagreements about the Bible are as much the symptoms as they are the causes of disunity. Not only is diversity possible but theory is less important than practice. Far more important than specific teachings or beliefs *about* the Bible is an actual, active engagement with the Bible's contents and the claims it makes on the lives of persons in the community of faith.

A worked-out view is important in order to discern appropriate implications and explain them to others but is not required in order to make the Scriptures significant for Christian living. On the contrary, individuals or groups can experience the claim of the scriptural message without thinking through all the ramifications involved in their approach to the Bible; they need not, in this sense, possess any *theory* of biblical authority. If persons can find the Bible useful without having any theory of its authority, then surely agreement among Christians about a single theory is not necessary either.

An Ecumenical Topic

Choosing to focus on the Bible may seem to be a peculiarly Protestant way of addressing the issue of authority, and in some ways it is. The Protestant slogan of "Scripture alone" has lent an inescapable urgency to the question of biblical authority which has often not been present in Roman Catholic or Eastern Orthodox circles. Observers are not surprised to find that every Protestant denomination has experienced internal disputes of one sort or another over the issue of scriptural authority. But despite the urgency and intensity with which Protestants have addressed the topic, scriptural authority is not exclusively a Protestant issue. The Roman Catholic Church has experienced its own conflicts regarding the topic. These erupted with particular force around the turn of the century, when Alfred Loisy's writings and those of other Roman Catholic modernists were under scrutiny. In 1907 "modernism" was defined and condemned by Pius X, and in 1908 Loisy was excommunicated. Not until 1943 were the prohibitions eased, and not until Vatican II (1962-65) was the full flowering of biblical study evident in Catholic circles. Whatever may have been true earlier, the past twenty years have witnessed a cooperative endeavor by Roman Catholics and Protestants to understand the Scriptures and apply them properly to contemporary life. Both traditions have the same need now for a coherent portrait of biblical authority. Since "two source" theories (where the two sources of church doctrine are Scripture and tradition) have been discredited in Roman Catholic circles and historical study has prompted Protestant scholars to acknowledge the important role of tradition, even the shape of the question is increasingly similar for Catholics and Protestants. The authority of the Bible is an issue that crosses denominational boundaries.

There is, of course, another sense in which scriptural authority is a topic on the ecumenical agenda. Interdenominational dialogues have moved toward mutual understanding by getting behind the divisive issues, searching for shared beliefs more basic than those that divide, and seeking a fresh approach to the topic under discussion. Sooner or later, this process of getting behind disagreements brings ecumenical dialogues back to the Scriptures, back to the Pauline understanding of justification,[1] for example, or back to Matthew 16 and the papacy, or back to several relevant New Testament passages that bear on the ordination of women. In every case the issue is not merely what the Scriptures say but what they mean in relation to contemporary developments. Any conclusion about their meaning is of necessity informed by some theory of biblical authority.

When ecumenical dialogues succeed, they usually produce a statement all parties can live with and on the basis of which a new level of cooperation and perhaps even a more organic union may be achieved. To substantiate the understanding of Christian identity found in such a statement appeals must be made to the Scriptures, and for this some theory of biblical authority is necessary. Biblical authority is an ecumenical topic, not only because the issue cuts across denominational boundaries but also because notions of authority influence ecumenical dialogue in crucial ways.

The Importance of Historical Criticism

Among churches involved in the ecumenical movement the discipline of historical criticism has been a helpful interpretive tool. Historical study has provided a nonconfessional, nondogmatic court of appeal to help adjudicate hitherto divisive issues of biblical interpretation. The methods of historical criticism are, however, currently under critique, and any contemporary theory of biblical authority must take the critique into account. Not only the traditionalists who oppose historical criticism but also its practitioners are now questioning its overall value, at least in the form it has been practiced since the nineteenth century. Brevard Childs, for example, believes that ascertaining the "degree of a narrative's historicity" or fixing the "age of a composition as somewhat older or somewhat younger" makes "little difference in one's total understanding of the literature." He therefore wonders whether it is possible "to break out of this sterile impasse and to enter into a *postcritical* era."[2] Childs believes that the usual historical-critical approach disregards the "religious dimension of the canon" when it assumes that political, social, and economic factors are the determining forces on every biblical text.[3] He challenges the assumption that "the theological point must be related to an original intention within the reconstructed historical context," arguing instead that the final, canonical form is normative.[4]

The very first sentence of a book by Walter Wink reads, "Historical biblical criticism is bankrupt."[5] The method, he goes on to argue, is "incommensurate with the intention of the texts," employs the false ideology of "objectivism," falls prey to "technologism," is "cut off from any community for whose life its results might be significant," and is, in the present context, "obsolete."[6]

Others join Wink and Childs in finding certain features of historical criticism unproductive. Though the criticisms vary, other charges in the indictment go something like this: By analyzing Scripture into separate pieces and focusing on their dissimilarity, historical criticism has rendered inaccessible any sense of the wholeness of the biblical message. By emphasizing the cultural and historical distance separating biblical times from our own day, historical criticism has robbed the reader of devotional immediacy. Moreover, the interpretation of biblical passages seems to hinge on such expertise as to leave church members intimidated and confused — so intimidated and confused as to ignore the Bible, gathering their values from here or there in the culture at large and no longer expecting from interpreters of the Bible any decisive guidance regarding faith and morals. Though some, such as Paul Ricoeur, advocate a postcritical "second immediacy" or "second naiveté,"[7] oth-

7

ers seem skeptical of its emergence, laying blame instead at the feet of historical criticism and its assumptions and practices.

Historical criticism is, of course, no one thing; it is a cluster of practices employed and applied in differing ways for differing purposes. In order to construct an integrated understanding of the authority of the Bible, one must evaluate the various historical-critical procedures to ascertain the range and limits of their usefulness. But in general, I find more to value in historical criticism than to condemn. However irrelevant to the church the specific endeavors of some biblical scholars may be and however much we may join their critics at some points, the overall attitude of this book toward historical criticism will be appreciative.

The Postmodern Setting

Any contemporary theory of biblical authority must take into account the character of its contemporary cultural context. This context is increasingly "postmodern." If, as I will argue in the next three chapters, modern culture was critical of authority, celebrating individual freedom and autonomy, postmodern culture so experiences the fragmentation and isolation which result from individualism that it hungers for a new sense of authority. If modern culture was sure of itself, postmodern society experiences a profound disorientation in which nothing seems to cohere and little seems to matter other than individual wants and desires. If modern culture was optimistic, postmodern culture lives more anxiously in the shadow of the mushroom-shaped cloud and the belching smokestacks of Auschwitz.

Western society in the twentieth century has moved more and more into a postmodern mode. Though cultural changes are gradual and impossible to date precisely, an awareness of the postmodern age dawned like a cymbal crash on some Europeans during and after World War I and drifted into every corner of American society during and after the Vietnam conflict.

This book will argue that theories of biblical authority have tended to employ modern assumptions that no longer count for much with persons influenced by a postmodern outlook. While acknowledging the complexity of gradual societal change, the book will seek to develop a theory of biblical authority less tied to modern assumptions and relatively more accessible to postmodern sensibilities.

No Contemporary Theological Consensus

Missing from our contemporary context is any overarching theological consensus. There was a time in the United States (say, in the late 1950s) when neo-orthodoxy provided the framework for much biblical study and theological reflection. After the trauma of World War I in Europe and the Great Depression in the United States, neo-orthodoxy reacted against "culture Protestantism." It viewed the Bible as the source of information not so much about the religious consciousness of human beings as about a qualitatively different God and about God's message to us as human beings. God's self-revelation was thought the basis for Christian theology, and this self-revelation was believed to be found in the Bible. The Bible, though not a textbook of doctrines, did offer an identifiably distinctive, relatively coherent pattern of thought. So long as neo-orthodoxy dominated theology, its view of revelation, God, and biblical theology could be assumed as the frame of reference within which to conduct more specialized studies and to make more specialized applications. The heyday of neo-orthodoxy is now past, and for better or worse, no other school of theology holds sway.

The declining influence of neo-orthodoxy means that little can be assumed in any constructive endeavor. Any scholar, pastor, or Christian layperson who would work with the Bible or theologize must in our day consciously clarify the view of biblical authority that informs that person's thinking. This book is intended neither to repudiate neo-orthodoxy nor to build upon it. It simply reflects a theological climate that is no longer neo-orthodox and that urgently needs to construct an integrated contemporary understanding of the Bible's authority.

The New Religious Right

During the past decade the new religious right has also entered the limelight. This movement is an understandable reaction to the disorientation of postmodern society. It endeavors to resuscitate old authority patterns that operated in premodern Christendom and in nineteenth-century "Protestant America," when Protestant values set the agenda for American society as a whole. The inescapable difficulty faced by the movement is that our society is now far less homogeneous than it was in the nineteenth century. No religious consensus exists to support the values endorsed by the new right. In order to prevail, those values would now have to be imposed. To undergird the kind of imposition needed, the Bible is enlisted as the bedrock authority. For the religious right the Bible thus functions in an *authoritarian* way—in being imposed contrary to community consensus—rather than as an *authority*. For just as biblical authority needs to be established over against the relativism and individualism of the postmodern era, so it must also

9

be distinguished from authoritarianism and from any triumphalistic perspective that attempts to impose itself on society as a whole.

It is vital for the future of us all that ways be found for Christian values to help humanize[8] our society, but it is equally important that Christian values not be imposed in an authoritarian manner. In a pluralistic society the Christian voice is one among others. Any proposal made by Christians can claim societal attention only because of, and to the degree of, its truth, its ethical sensitivity, and the integrity demonstrated by the community of faith. Christian proposals can only benefit from an ongoing debate with those who think differently, since debate keeps integrity and truth alive and prevents proposals from degenerating into expressions of only ideological and institutional self-interest. Because the Scriptures should not be imposed on society at large, their authority will need to be tied closely to the community of faith and its interaction with society as a whole.

The Constructive Task

A stirring manifesto on this topic which exuded confidence in its own correctness and its own ultimate significance would be exciting. But this is not to be. The task of the moment is not to lay down the gauntlet, demanding loyalty to one or the other side of an either/or, but to make connections and invite further thought.

Commitment to the gospel is needed today no less than at any other time in Christian history, but now more than ever we need to be clear about that to which we give our loyalty and we need to assess clearly what claims can rightly be made in its behalf. In a postmodern age nothing can be assumed and everything needs to be made explicit. In a postmodern age things are already disentangled and the pieces need to be put together again in ways that eschew bravado, in ways that do not lead again to disillusionment. Moreover, the theories that have been at odds with one another during the modern period are all out-of-date in the postmodern era. For the moment there is nothing to fight about; there is only a constructive task to be undertaken. If alternative ways to undertake this task exist, they are not yet clear enough to be divided into an either/or.

A book usually begins with claims regarding the crucial significance of the subject under discussion. As we have said, however, no particular *theory* of biblical authority is of central significance for Christian living. What *is* important is that the church be engaged with the Scriptures and make use of them. The community of faith serves God, the Scriptures serve the community of faith, and a theory of biblical authority assists in the rendering of this service. A theory of authority serves best when it generates an embodied message, engaged Bible study, and appropriate biblical interpretations.

The church is a community called into existence by God. In the church human beings encounter the divine call to serve God's purposes in the world. Here is also where they encounter the Scriptures. They discover that the Bible forms and informs the language and the identity of the community and shapes its image of God. It defines the "world" of the faithful as it is embodied in their lives. All of this occurs through usage—through ritual, praise, teaching, and prayer. Whatever else the Bible may accomplish, it serves the community and its purposes. Therefore the Scriptures function as an authority in the community before any theory describes their authority. The theory serves a practical end: the proper exercise of an already existing authority. The goal is to enable the Scriptures to function effectively as an actual authority in the life of the faithful. The purpose of the theory is not merely to enhance our understanding of the process but to equip us to engage in the process. The goal is an embodied message, nourished through engaged Bible study and appropriate methods of biblical interpretation.

Though not central, a good theory makes important contributions. Poor theories entangle and distract. Better theories illumine and release Christians to serve the kingdom more effectively. Like a crutch, an explicitly formulated theory is relatively more important in a crisis. Once one gets on with the walking again, the theory needs less attention. The transition to a postmodern cultural setting engenders a crisis within which the crutch must receive careful attention. This book is written in search of a better way to construe the many issues that come together in a contemporary, postmodern theory of biblical authority. Though the subject of the book is not in itself of crucial significance, it serves an activity that *is* crucial: the church's response to God's call and its service to the world. Because our topic is so closely related to this crucial activity, it is theologically urgent. We need to attend to it not for its own sake but so that we can get on with the basic task.

The Task in This Book

The overarching questions of the book are, What expectations can we appropriately bring to the Scriptures? What approach will allow the Bible its own integrity to challenge our ideas, priorities, and horizons? How can the texts be approached so as not to distort their meaning but to be fruitful for the faith of worshiping Christians today?

The discussion in the first three chapters is historical, but its purpose is not primarily to inform readers about the past. The description and analysis of the positions typically reflected in modern debates about the Bible are intended to permit readers to locate their own views and those of others with whom they are in contact. Six positions are described, of which four are considered to be viable. Each of these four ways of defending the authority of the Bible has its own integrity but also its own limitations. The persuasiveness of each is dependent on cultural assumptions now fast disappearing.

In the rest of the book, readers are invited to follow a thought process intended to stimulate their own thinking and help them nudge the thinking of others toward a more contemporary and more fully integrated understanding of the authority of the Bible. Some of the old but still currently discussed and defended arguments are left behind in favor of a contextual interpretation of scriptural passages within the community of faith. The approach I follow will not magically end all dispute, but it may move the discussion beyond unproductive arguments between incompatible theories of biblical authority and toward a productive focus on the recontextualized meaning of texts. If so, it will encourage the appropriate use of the Bible to nourish and sustain the church's service to the world.

Part One

The Modern Challenge
to Biblical Authority

1

Authority as Problematic in the Modern Era

If debate about the character and authority of the Scriptures has characterized the church in the modern period, the first question to be asked is why has this been so. A concise answer is possible. It is that there have been unique dynamics at work in the confrontation between Christianity and modern culture. Once stated, however, this answer demands elaboration. Chapter 1 will offer such elaboration and will address subsidiary questions: (1) What is modern culture? (2) What is the premodern background of the modern debate? (3) What effect did the church's confrontation with modern culture have on its own understanding of Scripture? Chapters 2 and 3 will delineate the range of positions that emerged as Christians sought to defend the authority of the Scriptures in the face of modern culture.

What Is Modern Culture?

As used here, *modern culture* is not the same as *contemporary culture*. The culture of our day may or may not be modern, because it remains in transition. In some ways and in some localities our society is still modern. In other ways and localities it is postmodern. (The term *postmodern* is vague enough to reveal some unclarity about what exactly is displacing modern culture. Some specific features of postmodern culture will be delineated in chap. 4.) Even aspects of the premodern may endure into the present day, but they are increasingly rare in the contemporary United States. The ubiquity of television is lethal to premodern cultural assumptions. In any case, more than one tendency is at work in contemporary society. By modern culture I will mean something more specific. *Modern culture* here designates a set of assumed values that dominated Western society from about 1700 until the twentieth century, persisting until World War I in Europe and until somewhat later—perhaps about 1960—in the United States. Modern values were originally associated with the Enlightenment and the Industrial Revolution. Because they were not so much defended as they were assumed as axioms by which to judge what was good and what was bad, the values are difficult to isolate and articulate. But despite the difficulty, a fairly well accepted portrait of modern culture is now available.[1]

A number of features of modern culture are important for our purposes:

Autonomous reason Though modern culture was in some ways a product of Christianity, it also sought independence from Christianity. Specifically, it appealed to reason rather than to faith as the basis for its ideas and its judgments. Reason was understood to be universal, to be as accessible to one person as to another—though not exercised equally by all, of course. To build on reason was to build on a foundation unbeholden to any particular social or religious group.

Negatively, there was an attempt to disentangle the faith-reason synthesis that had prevailed during the Middle Ages. People in the Middle Ages had endeavored to construct a culture and a society based on values and teachings drawn from Christianity. Reason, on the medieval approach, was correlated with faith: reason probed faith for its implications, reason drew inferences from the Christian faith, reason might even defend the Christian faith, but in no case was it to be autonomous. Religion was to be the foundation of society and its cohesive force.

Modern culture often portrayed the Middle Ages in very negative ways, ways now recognized to be inaccurate though understandable in light of the quite different priorities of the two periods. The Middle Ages were called the Dark Ages and were viewed as rife with superstition and ignorance. The modern age believed that unfettering reason from faith would lead to social betterment. That does not mean, of course, that advocates of modern culture were necessarily anti-Christian. In fact many of the early advocates were clergymen. But they either held a very universalized view of Christianity (Deism) or believed that both Christianity and culture would be better off if the two were disentangled.

Progress and antitradition Modern culture put a very positive value on progress. Progress became what it still is in the vocabulary of many, an unambiguously desirable thing. It was more and more often measured in quantifiable terms: technological innovations, a higher standard of living, a larger and larger gross national product, and the like. What were originally regarded as symptoms of more significant social betterment became the measure of progress and the focus of energies.

The society of the Middle Ages was pieced together slowly and laboriously out of the chaos that followed the fall of the Roman Empire. It thus prized stability and order. A positive value was placed on what was enduring. By contrast, modern culture tended to see continuity as a symptom of undesirable stagnation. Tradition was the specific target. Modern culture perceived fidelity to tradition to be the main source of stagnation. The Middle Ages had turned to the authorities of the past to illumine contemporary questions, but modern culture was apt to dismiss the past in favor of new solutions based on autonomous reason and empirical data. Innovation was believed the key to progress.[2]

As a historical religion, Christianity—like Judaism and Islam—roots its identity in traditions from the past. It relies on scriptural stories and historic creeds and doctrines for its self-understanding. The stance of modern culture against tradition thus posed a significant problem for Christianity. Either adjustments were necessary or the reliability of certain traditions needed to be defended.

Objectivity and the infatuation with science   Modern culture placed a high value on objectivity. Not only did it attempt to disentangle faith and reason, it also tried to disentangle the self from what was known about the world outside the self. Publicly verifiable knowledge based on observation and not dependent on the attitudes or responses of the self was regarded as objective. The high value placed on objectivity led to an infatuation with natural science. The prestige of natural science was inordinately high, and claims were made for it that went beyond what its limitations entitle. Any problem, many believed, could be solved if approached scientifically, and the pronouncements of scientists were to be heeded on almost any subject. Moreover, other disciplines attempted to copy the methods of natural science, to buttress their prestige by claiming for themselves scientific status. This was true of experimental psychology (now regarded no longer as a branch of philosophy but as a separate discipline), positivism in philosophy, and some late-nineteenth-century liberal theology, to cite but three examples.

Values, whatever their objective components and consequences, are incapable of objective verification. Who, for example, can prove *objectively*—that is, by observing empirical data and analyzing the data mathematically—that it is better to love one's neighbor than to protect one's own interests? Therefore the quest for objectivity meant that value-oriented questions were either neglected or relegated to the status of unsubstantiated private opinions. Society lived on the capital of value commitments inherited from earlier epochs.

Value commitments are intrinsic to Christianity: loving one's neighbor is better than behaving selfishly, obeying God is of a higher priority than obeying political authorities, human life is more valuable than property, and so on. Relegating these values to secondary status privatized the Christian faith, threatened the cultural self-confidence of Christians, and limited their social impact. Whereas the values of

17

Christianity had for centuries been honored as self-evident, now their validity seemed at best ambiguous. The uncertain footing of Christian values caused anxiety within the church and among its spokespersons.

The quest for objectivity also entailed a psychic tension for any who remained committed to Christianity. The tension stemmed from the divergent roles expected of the self. In order to achieve objectivity, the self has to detach itself from what it is exploring. The self becomes an observer, cultivating neutrality and extirpating interestedness of any sort that would prejudice the results of the investigation. By contrast, Christianity prizes involvement of the self, in trust and hope, in faith and love. What Christianity promises is a deeper understanding, which comes as the self lives out the faith and explores its implications. In contemporary terminology, Christianity is more praxis (that is, theorizing amid active involvement and in the light of concrete commitments) than detached investigation or abstract theorizing. The tension thus created in the Christian's psyche arises from the strain between detachment and involvement. The temptation then is to reduce the tension even when inappropriate, by cultivating detachment all around—with a devastating effect not only on the self's Christian commitment but also on all human relationships of any depth. Or the tension can be reduced by claiming for Christianity some element of objectivity that matches the objectivity claimed for other knowledge. Such objectivity was laid claim to, for example, by those who sought to locate the essence of Christianity through historical analysis[3] and by others who ascribed scientific accuracy to the biblical documents.[4]

Optimism Modern culture prized human potential. A good deal of optimism existed concerning what human beings could do if only the chains of superstition and prejudice were removed. The modern age thus concentrated its efforts on education, not just for the ruling elite but for everyone, in the belief that educated persons would automatically choose the good. The idea of perfectibility through education, however, was at odds with the Christian emphasis on the inextricably sinful tendencies of human beings.

Individualism Modern culture exalted the autonomous individual. Each individual was thought to possess within his or her own self-sufficient rationality the ability to discover the truth, know the good, and make informed moral judgments. Given the high value placed on objective knowing, entanglements of any kind were suspect. Given the disparagement of tradition, any authority that demanded loyalty to inherited ideas and institutions was equally suspect. Given the high value placed on objective knowing, symbols and rituals were regarded either as superfluous or as unfortunate in their influence. Individual

18

initiative, individual judgment, individual autonomy—these were all highly regarded and pursued.

The effect was to diminish the role of communal support and to ignore the importance of human community in all its various forms. A tension was consequently introduced between the practice of Christianity—which typically meant involvement in the community of faith through worship and service—and theoretical interpretations of Christianity that viewed faith as if it were an individual decision arrived at through individual experience or isolated contemplation of a text, through meditation on the mysteries of the universe or contemplation of the moral law within, or through induction from objective data.

Mechanism   For the most part, modern culture operated with a mechanical view of the universe. The world was pictured as one gigantic machine, with every part mechanically related to every other part. *A* caused *B*, *B* caused *C*, and so on. Even more significant was the attendant idea that to describe the totality of causal linkages would be exhaustively to describe natural developments.

To some degree a mechanical view of the universe was the result of Christian influence. The world had been desacralized by the first creation account, in Gen. 1:1—2:3,[5] and by subsequent developments in Jewish and Christian understanding. But a mechanical universe was a thoroughly desacralized universe, one still more desacralized than any imagined or portrayed by the biblical authors.

What is more, the mechanistic view created difficulties for Christianity in its endeavor to understand the biblical narratives. The biblical narratives offered explanations that from the standpoint of a mechanistic view of the world seemed to appeal to extraneous causes, whether to angels, or the miraculous power of an individual, or God's own rulership. Did the apparently extraneous causes have any effect at all? Did they intrude upon the natural causal order and cause a suspension of it? Did they supplement the natural causal order? Satisfactory answers were difficult to find.

Although other features of modern culture could be identified, these six closely interrelated characteristics are sufficient for our purposes. Despite how things at times looked, the overall effect of modernity was not to create an all-out war between Christianity and culture but to introduce a new set of tensions and anxieties. Christianity, for the first time since it had been adopted as the official religion of the Roman Empire, was confronted with an autonomous set of cultural values. These values were simultaneously enticing and problematic for anyone committed to Christianity.

The Premodern Background

Christian theology did not encounter modern culture empty-handed. Its response was shaped by its own traditions and the positions it had hammered out during previous centuries. Throughout the history of the church, the Bible has been regarded as the ultimate norm for Christian teaching. Despite misinterpretations that picture the medieval church as subordinating or neglecting the authority of the Bible, in fact the authority of the Bible was never really eclipsed and never really in doubt. The arguments of the pre-Reformation and Reformation periods concerned the right to interpret the Bible and the importance of other voices in the life of the church. They were not arguments that questioned the authority of the Bible itself. Neither Roman Catholics nor Protestants doubted the central importance of the Scriptures for doctrine, faith, and Christian living.

The overall development went something like this. An underlying assumption prevailed during the Middle Ages that the Bible, church tradition (especially the writings of the fathers), church authority (especially papal authority), and reason (philosophy) all spoke with a unified voice. Tradition was questioned first: doubts were introduced not so much about its importance as about its uniformity. Abélard and others identified contradictions among the church fathers, and the schoolmen (the theologians of the emerging universities) labored hard to overcome these discrepancies. Thomas Aquinas, for example, in each article of his *Summa Theologiae* cited contradictory opinions from the tradition as a preliminary to his own resolution of the point under discussion. Yet, despite the best efforts of the schoolmen, confidence that church tradition could settle arguments gradually diminished. Dialectics—that is, the use of reason as a tool for exhibiting the coherence of theology and for eliciting the correct implications of its postulates—began to gain in importance. This was to some degree an unintended consequence but a consequence all the same.

Next to be questioned was ecclesiastical authority. In the fourteenth and fifteenth centuries the performance of popes and councils was sufficiently scandalous to decrease confidence in their capacity to represent authentic Christianity and to settle disputes fairly. Europe saw rival popes claiming legitimacy and councils arriving at contradictory decisions. Circumstances conspired to produce Renaissance popes who seemed more interested in the fine arts, martial arts, and power politics than in theology and spiritual leadership. The reasons were extremely complex, of course, but the net result was diminished confidence in ecclesiastical authority.

The alliance between reason and theology was loosened at the same time. A marvelously nuanced synthesis between faith and reason had been forged by the High Middle Ages, and the philosophy used in this synthesis had been drawn either from Plato or from Aristotle. The classical philosophies were now gradually replaced by nominalism, which denied the reality of universals and conceded the reality only of individuals. It held that the mind could only generalize or draw conclusions from actual perceptible occurrences; it could not comprehend the rational structure of things and therefore could not make valid speculative inferences. Consequently, it could not claim to understand God. As nominalism gained acceptance, it disrupted the earlier synthesis of faith and reason. Many claims that had been made and many congruities that had been located now seemed less self-evident. The tendency among those influenced by nominalism was to appeal to revelation as an independent authority that was to be accepted on faith. Reason, they held, could work out the implications of revelation but could not provide an independent justification for theological claims: the explanations for what had been revealed were hidden within the inscrutable will of God.

As dialectics had gained in significance at the expense of tradition, so revelation now gained at the expense of philosophy. With decreased confidence in reason, revelation stood alone as the sole theological authority. And directly related to revelation was the record of revelation: the Scriptures. The Bible was believed to record the actual results of God's will, the actual choices God had made from among many options.[6]

A lower regard for reason, church tradition, and ecclesiastical authority left the Scriptures as the only authority to emerge unscathed. As esteem for the others went down, the relative esteem for Scripture's authority went up, even if the claims made in its behalf remained in themselves unchanged.

All of this occurred prior to the Reformation, so that Luther inherited a theological tradition that, for all practical purposes, operated with the principle of "Scripture alone." No other authority was Scripture's equal. In the *via moderna* of his teachers little confidence existed that reason, church authority, and tradition would speak with one voice; Scripture could be played off against them or any one of them played off against the others. To the degree that the Reformation added anything new on this issue, it was to stake out for itself one new area, namely, that of the authority to interpret the Scriptures. Whereas Roman Catholics as a rule held together the Scriptures and the body of scriptural interpretation that had been developed over the centuries, the Reformation came to set the Scriptures over against the received opinion about them. The Reformation claimed a breakthrough in biblical interpretation such that its own interpretation called into question many of the inherited commonplaces. Luther, for example, read the Scriptures *coram Deo*, that is, in terms of what they said to the individual or the community face to face with God. The Bible for him was not simply the archival source of doctrines, it was a living communication that was not properly Word until it was effectively communicated and internalized by human beings.[7] Its impact on human beings was understood through the dialectic of law and gospel, and that dialectic became an important interpretive tool in his challenge against the scholastic understanding of the Bible.

Moreover, the Reformation as a whole tended to make use of the expertise in languages and textual criticism which had been achieved during the Renaissance. Following the humanists "back to the sources," the Reformers disentangled the Bible from the interpretive overlay of the intervening centuries. In the Greek text (in contrast to its Latin translation), for example, *metanoieite* could not mean "do penance" but could only mean "repent." This crucial word was a call to reorient one's life rather than an encouragement to participate in the medieval penitential system. With this one change a whole body of scholastic commentary fell.

Thus the post-Reformation debates developed into debates between rival ways of interpreting the Scriptures. Though Roman Catholics remained loyal to the papacy and Protestants did not, though Roman Catholics defended Scripture and tradition over against the Protestant battle cry of "Scripture alone," though the Roman Catholic hierarchy claimed the right to interpret Scriptures and denied this right to individuals, though the Bible played a different role in the popular piety of Protestants than in that of Roman Catholics, and though many other minor differences clouded the picture, there was yet no fundamental disagreement about the superior status of the Bible, its inspiration, or its normative role in the church. The polemical and didactic theologies developed by the Roman Catholics, the Lutherans, and the Reformed during the post-Reformation period all assumed, without defense, that the Scriptures formed the common court of appeal.

The theology of all three traditions was didactic because the distinctiveness of each tradition needed to be explained clearly. People needed to understand what it meant to be a Lutheran or a Calvinist or a Roman Catholic and needed to be persuaded that it made some difference. Only then would the insights of each particular tradition be preserved. In most cases both theological loyalty and political unity were at stake. The theology of the three traditions was also polemical. Polemics reinforced the distinctiveness of each tradition and helped persuade persons that it deserved to be maintained. Polemics endeavored to prove one position and disprove the others by appeal to authority, and the one major authority recognized by all parties was the Bible.

Two consequences followed. The first was that the Bible was treated as if it were a theological textbook containing the axioms and theorems from which doctrinal implications could be drawn. Though inspiration had not been a factor of immediate and direct importance in determining the canon of the Christian Bible,[8] post-Reformation theology appealed to the doctrine of inspiration as the foundational justification for employing the Scriptures as a sourcebook for doctrine. If the Bible was the inspired Word of God, then it contained supernaturally authenticated information from which theological deductions were possible.

What happened therefore was that a magnificent theological edifice was gradually built, one that had as its only acknowledged foundation the Scriptures understood in ahistorical, textbook fashion. Of course, other assumptions drawn from outside the Bible—assumptions about the changeless character of God, for example, or assumptions about human nature—did enter post-Reformation theology, but these were seldom acknowledged to be extrabiblical and therefore remained largely unnoticed. Even persons who claimed not to put much stock in tradition were so influenced by the tradition that the extrabiblical assumptions seemed self-evident to them.

Though what I say here is most obviously true for Protestant theology (Lutheran orthodoxy and Calvinist orthodoxy), it is with but one modification true also for Roman Catholic theology. For Roman Catholics, at least up through the Council of Trent, inspiration was not limited to the written Scriptures but extended to scriptural interpretation within the church.[10] While influencing the content of some judgments, this extension did not really disrupt the basic agreement of Roman Catholics and Protestants concerning the inspiration of the Bible. For interpretation was still interpretation *of the Bible;* the Bible was understood to be a textbook. Each theological edifice still rested essentially on the same foundation, even if Protestantism linked theological conclusions more directly and immediately to the Bible than Roman Catholicism did with its emphasis on the tradition of interpretation. (We have here an instance of how much alike polemical adversaries often are or become in the course of their disputes.)

The second consequence was that the authority of the Bible was *assumed.* It was not defended, because it did not need to be defended.

The groups that were locked in polemical battle did not differ at this point. Because the two non-Christian religions with whom people in Europe were acquainted—Judaism and Islam—both had highly prized Scriptures, when the Christian Scriptures were defended the defense most often took the form of an argument in favor of Christian writings over against those approved by Jews and Muslims. The more radical question of why a person should appeal to Scriptures at all was never asked, because there was no reason to ask it.[11]

Not only was the Bible's authority for theology and doctrine regarded as axiomatic, its authority for culture and society was also assumed. The Bible provided the values upon which a culture should be built. Though the particular judgments about the shape society should take differed and though disagreements persisted about how one should move from the Bible to the proper societal implications, there was no disagreement about the importance and authority of the Bible in this area. The post-Reformation period remains within the chronicle of Christendom. Not until the American Revolution and the unique circumstances under which a national government needed to be created on the North American continent did mainline churches seriously entertain notions of the separation of church and state. By then the values of modern culture were already available to provide the intellectual framework for conceiving the separation.

The Effect of Modern Culture on the Understanding of Scripture

Modern culture offered a new and thoroughgoing challenge, not because the authority of the Bible was directly denied but because it was no longer assumed. Scriptural authority for the first time needed to be defended in some way, and its defense needed to employ terms and appeal to priorities that made sense when judged by the criteria of modern culture and its values.

The required defense turned out to be an exceedingly delicate undertaking, because the values held highest by modern culture were in many cases at odds with those operating within Christianity. A person either had to appeal to the values of modern culture in a theological prolegomenon that buttressed the authority of the Bible and then to develop the specifically Christian values out of a subsequent analysis of the Bible, or had to subject the entire world view of modern culture to a more or less thoroughgoing critique, construct a revision, and then posit a more harmonious relationship between the revised cultural values and Christianity. In either case, the situation was precarious: one had to walk the precipice between an all-out endorsement of modern culture, to the neglect of Christian values, and an all-out involvement in a religious world divorced from the vitalities of culture as a whole. A few thinkers, properly called modernists, chose to endorse modern culture (virtually none of the theologians whom conservative polemists labeled modernists were in this group), and a few chose to withdraw from modern culture altogether (the old Order Amish being among the most intriguingly consistent in this regard), but the majority of theologians walked the precipice and defended the Scriptures in one way or another. In the next two chapters we will look at the several ways in which they did this.

In any case, Christianity encountered a new challenge—new at least for Christendom, new at least for Western Europe since the conversion of the "barbarian" tribes—for which a theological response needed to be constructed. Various groups within Christianity formulated different responses, each appealing to different facets of the value system of modern culture. The arguments about the Bible in the modern period have largely occurred between these groups, each claiming that its defense was the best and each believing that nothing less than the credibility of the Bible was at stake. Every defense, including that of the fundamentalists, has been a *modern* defense, arising during the modern period, appealing to modern assumptions, and seeking to respond to a peculiarly modern question. Each of the responses has employed materials drawn from church tradition, but because church tradition supplies no ready-made answers to the modern challenge, each position has needed to be fashioned anew. Those who claimed to represent "the unaltered tradition" were employing an anachronism.[12]

Although every defense of the Scriptures constructed by Christians was in one way or another modern, none of those that we will subsequently judge viable was modernist, because none endorsed the values of modern culture completely. In this way fundamentalists, premillennialists, and other "countermoderns" are as much moderns as are those who employ historical criticism in a responsible fashion,[13] and the liberals who make use of historical criticism are as much conservatives—in following the tradition—as are those who call themselves that.

Christian endeavors to defend the authority of the Scriptures over against the priorities of modern culture were not aided by the social situation in which theologians operated. Socially, the Bible was often used to buttress regimes and laws and institutions dedicated to preserving the status quo or restoring what had been the status quo prior to one or another social revolution—especially, of course, the French Revolution. Advocates of social reform often found themselves faced with biblical as well as political, economic, and social arguments. In such circumstances it was tempting for social reformers, motivated essentially by a sense of justice, to polemize against the Bible[14] or against those positions claiming the support of the Bible.[15] Christians in sympathy with social reform found themselves caught in the middle. They were forced to explain how they could endorse the reforms and the rationale offered for those reforms—which appealed to the values of modern culture—while still accepting the authority of the Bible.

Among the reactionary groups who opposed reform there was the need, as the arguments developed and the differing assessments of the Bible emerged, to defend the Scriptures in ways that made sense to those imbued with modern culture. And Christians who did not share the reactionary views—who were, for example, more in the middle of the road politically—were obliged to do the same. They had to construct a defense of biblical authority that enabled them to explain how they could appeal to the Bible and still not endorse the social consequences the reactionaries claimed to find mandated there.[16]

In other instances, especially later in the modern period, advocates of social reform themselves sometimes appealed to the Scriptures. As in the case of the middle-of-the-road Christians, they needed to explain how they approached and interpreted the Scriptures so as to emerge with conclusions about social policy so at odds with the reactionaries'.

Thus the complicated social situation increased the urgency of clarifying the status of the Scriptures, but it also increased the passion with which disagreements were argued. For many, not merely a theological position but a whole social program seemed at stake. And for those convinced that their particular social program was the remedy for the ills of their nation, the volcano-like emotions of nationalism also became involved.

But as important as the complications are, the underlying tension was created by modern culture itself. In order to underline the challenge to biblical authority presented by modern culture, especially given the heritage of post-Reformation (sixteenth- and seventeenth-century) theology, we will return to the features of modern culture that I have already identified.

Autonomous reason The autonomy of modern culture and its appeal to reason had two consequences. One is by now obvious. The authority of the Bible and Christian values could not be assumed but needed to be justified. Any defense involved appeals to some of the assumptions at work in modern culture. The second consequence was that Christianity had to sort out its attitude toward reason, because reason now meant something quite different from what it had meant before. For modern culture what was reasonable was what was in principle, even if not in fact, universally self-evident to any observer or to anyone who had the correct information. For premodern Christendom what had been reasonable was what followed logically from Christian assumptions or was congruent with them. Many claims to reasonableness made by traditional Christian theology were challenged by modern culture, because the criterion of reasonableness had changed.

One marvelous illustration of this is Anselm's ontological argument for the existence of God. In his *Proslogium*, Anselm offers the argument as part of a prayer addressed to God, to the very God whose existence he wants to "prove"![17] In the modern period this argument was often discussed without reference to its setting.[18] It was then either dismissed, because its assumptions were not universal or not sufficiently neutral, or revised to reflect the new situation.

Anyone in the modern period who supported the authority of the Scriptures had to defend by appeal to standards of universal, self-sufficient reason a document written "from faith to faith" (Rom. 1:17 KJV). To the degree that Christianity could be endorsed by universal reason, it seemed to lose its distinctiveness. To the degree that its uniqueness was upheld, it seemed unreasonable and inherently provincial and elitist. The question of the uniqueness of Christianity was unavoidable and was addressed in one way or another by every one of the several defenses of biblical authority constructed during the modern period.

Progress and antitradition Appeals to the Bible were appeals to the past. To modern culture these seemed intrinsically reactionary, inherently against progress. This feature of modern culture posed the most direct challenge to Christianity of any I have described. In the first place, it directly challenged the very foundation on which post-Reformation theologies had been built: the undisputed authority of the Bible. The culturally acknowledged foundation provided by the Bible seemed to be rejected out of hand in favor of the priorities of modern culture. Without discrimination, what was past was suspect, including the post-Reformation textbook for Christian theology, the Bible.

What is even more serious, post-Reformation theology was tied so closely to the Bible that its own theological propositions were often seen to represent the very content of the Christian faith. Its own theology did not claim to interpret the Bible so much as to summarize in more orderly form the Bible's doctrinal contents. The necessary distinc-

27

tion between the content of revelation and the human act of theologizing had become obscured. A later orthodox theologian such as Abraham Calov could even speak of "revealed theology."[19] Doctrine and theology were not just based on revelation, they were contained in and part of revelation. Here the challenge of modern culture created not just a theological crisis but a crisis of faith, because to disturb the theology was to tamper with revelation. (And so it continues to seem to twentieth-century heirs of post-Reformation theology: thus the anxiety created by historical criticism or anything else that requires theological reformulation.)

In the second place, the bias against tradition found in modern culture directly challenged the core of Christianity. Liberals and conservatives alike needed to respond to the challenge on this level. Since the Christian faith was based on revelatory acts of God is *history*, especially the life, death, and resurrection of Jesus the Christ, the very possibility of Christian faith seemed under challenge. It could not be sustained without some importance being ascribed to certain crucial events of the past.

The Christian response was to defend the importance of tradition, meaning the authority and importance of what happened in the past. The defense was carried out essentially in one of two ways: either by defending a uniform, unchanging static tradition (see chap. 2) or by defending a dynamic, developing tradition, conceived on an organic model (see chap. 3). The dynamic view allowed its advocates to acknowledge real progress but not at the expense of abandoning the past. The static view minimized progress—though often not denying it altogether—while defending what had come from the past. Frequently what the static view also minimized was the "pastness" of the tradition, that is, its difference from the present. The continuity between past and present was overestimated.

Objectivity and the infatuation with science One challenge was to clarify the character of what is recorded in the Scriptures. Does the Bible provide objective information? If so, is this information to be corrected by objective information gathered according to modern scientific procedures? Another challenge was to clarify the epistemological status of values and to clarify the role of the self.

Optimism Since it was believed that human improvement was through the use of unfettered reason, the question arose how the Bible's authority could be conceived so as not to fetter human beings once more. How could one specify precisely what things of value the Bible would add to human lives?

Individualism The challenge here was two-sided. Of what use was the Bible? Where was it useful? If the Bible was in fact useful only in the community of faith, then it seemed to have no objective authority and no authority for culture and society as a whole. If, on the other hand, its authority extended to culture and society, then it seemed to impose restrictions on the autonomy of individuals in society.

Mechanism The credibility of the biblical witness depended on its assertion that God has caused certain things in human history to happen. God was involved causatively in the exodus, in the giving of the Torah, in the words of the prophets, in Jesus, and in the deeds of the faithful. Only because of this are certain historical events revelatory and Christian confidence justified. But a mechanical view of the universe seemed to exclude any special causal involvement by God in events and thereby to exclude God's special grace. On the mechanical view, the only way God could act was through universally applicable natural laws. The challenge posed by modern culture was that of reconciling competing views of the universe. For the Bible, everything was under the personal and immediate supervision of God. On the modern view, God seemed to be excluded.

The advent of modern culture confronted the church with a basic apologetic task: it needed to formulate a defense of the Bible and its authority.

2

Responses within a Static
World View

The next step is to discuss the effects of the several points of tension between Christianity and modern culture on the church's understanding of the authority of the Bible. How did that tension influence the shape of modern debates about the Bible? In what ways did Christians respond to the challenge of modern culture?

My thesis is that the quarrels about the Bible were largely quarrels between different factions within Christianity, each advocating one possible way of responding to the tension and each defending the status of the Bible over against modern culture. Because post-Reformation theology—and Protestant piety—had assumed the Bible's authority as its starting point, modern culture provoked a significant theological crisis that demanded resolution. Christians sought to respond to the crisis in several ways, and the quarrels about the Bible that occurred in the church were primarily between groups that advocated different responses to the cultural challenge. These groups often lost sight of the apologetic task and focused their energies on battling one another.

The partisans of any one position often asserted that theirs represented church tradition and that others succumbed in one way or another to modern culture. This they did despite the fact that their position differed from the others only in the way it understood and defended the tradition and the points at which it made contact with modernity. Each group claimed that its own position captured *the* biblical view of authority, whereas in fact all the positions made extrabiblical appeals.

Six general positions figure in the debate, each constituting one rival attempt to defend the Bible against the challenges its authority faced in the modern world: rationalism, supernaturalism, evangelicalism, ecclesial developmentalism, analogical developmentalism, and dynamic humanism. The first three will be explained and analyzed in this chapter, and the remaining three will be discussed in chapter 3.

Several key features distinguish one position from another. These features, however, do not constitute an exhaustive list of what could be noticed. The six positions reflect a schematized pattern, and no claim is made that their key features account for every possible variation. The six positions are general models; they are nothing more than convenient analytic devices whose inexact formulation, if imprecision occurs, will not jeopardize the overall argument.

"Types" of Christian Response

The schematized pattern is not intended to be a set of pigeon-holes for categorizing various thinkers and theologians. Among other things, it is too incomplete for that purpose. To be sure, the various positions are not merely hypothetical. Specific historical thinkers exemplify each and will be mentioned in the course of the discussion, but these persons and their theologies are not what are under analysis here. My intention is instead to uncover the dynamics of Christian thought as that thought encountered modern culture and responded to the discrepancies between its values and the church's allegiance to scriptural authority. We need to know what forces were at work, and what major variations emerged as Christians wrestled with the forces. We need to see the logic and the contextual purpose of the various positions in order to evaluate their significance. Individual theologians may have modified or combined the positions described here or may even have constructed new alternatives while wrestling with the same forces and still appealing to specifically modern assumptions.

Of the conclusions that my analysis will yield, two are of central significance. The first is that each position was influenced by the context in which it was developed, a context reflecting the need to sort out Christian identity in the face of modern culture. Each is therefore viable on its own terms only so long as modern cultural values remain influential. As the context changes, the whole issue must be reevaluated by the contemporary church. The second conclusion is that each position employs assumptions or makes theological assertions that influence the way the Bible is understood but that are not mandated by the Bible itself. For want of a better phrase, I will call these extrabiblical considerations. My term by no means implies that they are antibiblical; it implies only that their source is an imaginative construal[1] that is not itself drawn from the Bible. Even if an image from the Bible is used in the imaginative construal, it is but one of several images found there and the decision to give it central importance is based on extrabiblical considerations.

The most basic component of extrabiblical imaginative construals is a unified portrait of how God relates to the world and to its patterns of cause and effect. Another component is a specific notion of what constitutes religious knowledge. Still another is a particular understanding of change and continuity as these affect the history of God's people. These components and others are gathered together into

a single, composite image—an extrabiblical imaginative construal—
that informs the theory of authority found in each modern defense of
the Bible.

Three of the six positions I will discuss work within a developmentalist understanding of the past. The basic image for the developmentalist is evolutionary growth and decay. The metaphors are often
organic. Just as an acorn grows into an oak tree, so does everything
change: ideas, dress, economic relationships, mores, tools, scientific
theories, tastes, political boundaries, and even definitions of what it
means to be human. God may or may not be subject to change, but at
least the human perceptions of God change, along with every other
aspect of human culture. All such changes must be taken into account
when interpreting a text or locating continuity or claiming authorization from the past for some position taken in the present. The developmentalist model does not, of course, postulate random change. Just as
an acorn always yields an oak tree and never a maple, so some basic
continuities exist in human history. Amid the changes, recognizable
patterns of intelligibility can be found. The unique identity of each
individual and each group can be seen amid their many transformations.

The other three positions, those which will be discussed in the
present chapter, view the past as static. Though superficial changes
admittedly abound in history, this model postulates an essential,
unchanging core. God can act, but God does not change. Though human
beings do not dress the same or use the same tools from one epoch to
another, human nature remains constant. The patriarchs do not differ
fundamentally from contemporary persons of faith. The accouterments
of culture change, but the basic virtues and foibles of human beings
expressed therein do not. At some fundamental level an unchanging
essence persists behind or beneath the superficial exterior. Not only is
God unchanging, the truth about God remains constant and expressions of that truth need no reformulation.

Two of the six positions I discuss fall outside the sphere of Christian self-understanding. Though not without religious virtue, these two
positions are not viable options for Christians who wish to understand
rather than reject the authority of the Bible. In order to have authority
a document needs to be able to make claims on the attention of the
Christian community. The viable options define the role of the Bible in
such a way as to preserve its ability to make such claims. The other two
positions do not; they subsume biblical insights under the authority of
present understanding or of present aspirations for the future. The Bible
can then only endorse claims made in other ways and from other sources;
it is not accorded the right to make claims running counter to the other

authority. (This does not imply that subscribing to one of the two positions automatically makes a person a non-Christian; it implies only that the position is unworkable for the church as a whole.)

These two positions (the first and last to be discussed) are included in my list for three reasons: (1) I want to show that both the developmental and the static models, if understood in certain ways, can fall outside the boundaries of a viable Christian theology. Neither model is inherently safe or inherently dangerous. (2) Including the positions can help explain some mistaken arguments. Those holding a position based on either the static or the dynamic model have often incorrectly accused those working with a position based on the other model of succumbing to the unacceptable position associated with that model. (3) A knowledge of the two unacceptable positions can help us understand more clearly the dynamics at work in the four remaining positions.

Of the four remaining positions, two employ a static model of history and two employ a developmentalist model. The most fundamental, implacable difference between positions involves the choice of one or the other of these models—a choice based on extrabiblical considerations.

The Rationalist Position

The rationalist position operates with a static view of the past, endorses the assumptions of modern culture, and undercuts the authority of the Bible.[2]

One premodern way to construe the relationship between God and the world was to think of God as a person with a hands-on control of everything that happened. Because God actively directed the winds, no particular conceptual problem was created when God was said to change the direction of the wind or decrease its velocity, whether at the Reed Sea or the Sea of Galilee. A miracle was as simple as moving the pen in my hand in a different direction or increasing its pace across the page. No natural laws were broken, because modern conceptions of natural law were not part of this premodern portrait of God's relationship to the world.

Another, somewhat different, premodern view depicted the world as a large house, divided into a supernatural "upstairs" and a realm of nature "downstairs." On this view laws were at work in nature, so that one event caused another to happen and God was not in direct and immediate control of every natural phenomenon. But God did orchestrate the whole and did continue to cause and to influence directly at least some of the events. Though the relationship between the two floors in the house was understood in a variety of ways, few barriers separated nature and supernature. Exchange was free, open, and frequent. Angelic messengers appeared and theophanies occurred as the supernatural visited the downstairs, and mystical visions and ecstatic experiences gave humans a glimpse of the upstairs. Because no barriers were perceived to separate the floors, prayers addressed to God for alterations downstairs caused no conceptual problems. God could influence the surroundings as well as converse with those who lived on the ground floor.

Mechanism   The modern world came to conceive the natural order as a vast machine. For it every movement had an antecedent, natural cause somewhere in the machine. And that cause in turn had another, and so on. The universe was thus one complex network of causes and effects, and any interruption of the operating machine was an almost unthinkably complex operation. To halt temporarily the sun's apparent movement around the earth, for example, the entire universe would have to be stopped for a time, the planets would have to be held in place without the equilibrium of gravity and centrifugal force which at present maintains their orbits, and the whole machinery would have to be restarted with such precision as to resume movements identical with those which would have occurred without the interruption. It became exceedingly difficult to imagine that all this would be done to help one individual or one tiny band of people trying to conquer the promised land.[3]

Except for God the only thing lying outside the causal machinery was the freedom of the human self—if indeed any such freedom existed that was not illusory. (This matter came under extensive debate, especially with the rise of the social sciences, when various philosophies of determinism challenged the older assumptions of personal freedom.) It remained a puzzle how human freedom could influence the causal order, but the rationalists are quite sure that freedom is able to do so as long as it respects the natural and moral laws that govern the world's machinery. Whatever the limitations of national agents, they possess freedom enough to cause some things to happen.[4]

Apart from allowing scope to human freedom, then, the rationalists endorse the mechanistic view of the world found in modern culture and reject anything that seems to contradict it. Miracles, defined as interruptions of the causal order, are ruled out, explained away, or at least, regarded as of dubious authenticity and value.

For the rationalist, the universe still exhibits a first and a second story, but a barrier is now perceived to separate the two floors. A pattern of cause and effect holds sway downstairs to such a degree that free and frequent interaction is no longer possible between the super-natural and the natural. God does not have hands-on control but governs only through natural (and moral) law. God's last immediate involvement occurred at creation. This does not necessarily mean that God has since then been absent or totally inactive, but it entails that divine activity is always channeled through universally applicable laws.

The task for human beings is to abide by the moral law and the natural law. Those who disobey the natural law—by trying to fly off a tall building, for example—reap the consequences of injury and death. Those who disobey the moral law likewise reap the consequences of eternal punishment. Rewards will be given to those who freely obey. God does not give special assistance (grace) to individual human beings and does not grant special revelations to individual groups of people. What is available is available to all without favoritism or prejudice.[5] Thus the rationalists endorse the universality valued by modern culture. What is true religiously is true for everyone everywhere and in principle accessible to them through the use of unaided reason.

Optimism   The rationalists endorse modernity's high view of human potential. For them sin is not so great an impediment as to need a special atonement. Education is necessary, to be sure, but human beings remain free to follow the moral law if they but will. When the moral law is followed, life will surely improve.

Individualism   The rationalists also endorse the modern notion of the autonomous individual. Each person has to decide whether to use reason or not, whether to behave in a moral way or not. No special role is ascribed to community ties or to symbols, which are viewed with suspicion. Rituals and ceremonies are superfluous and deleterious additions to religion, invented by priests who need to multiply religious requirements in order to retain a role for themselves and their services. True worship is virtuous living, an individual responsibility that can be borne by no one else.

Progress and antitradition   Progress, too, the rationalists value. Imbued with the optimism of the Enlightenment and the Industrial Revolution, rationalists believe reason can gain new insight into the workings of the world and thereby improve the economic and moral state of society. The main obstacles to progress are superstition and ignorance. Therefore education is the key, in both the social and religious realm. Jesus and the other great religious teachers were precisely that: teachers. They added nothing that reason could not in principle discern on its own, but they aided reason in its task.

Not only is education important, so is freedom. Inherited authorities are suspect, because their principles and perspectives seem to be discredited by empirical investigation and to retard progress and insight. Religious authorities are suspect no less than any others. Reason should take a critical stance, a posture of detached doubt, toward external authority of any kind, and specifically toward the Bible, which needs to be scrutinized to discover where it does and does not measure up to reason.

Thus the rationalists endorse the antitradition stance of modern culture as well. Depending on the temperament and social context of the individual rationalist, church tradition can be honored as beneficial for the unenlightened who need it or lampooned as sheer superstition, but in either case it is accorded no independent authority. As part of the church tradition—that is, as part of the inheritance from the past—the Scriptures receive either genteel respect or detailed critique. Their contents are significant only when independently confirmed by reason: the Scriptures have no other claim on modern persons.

The famous case of Thomas Jefferson's cutting out the moral teachings of Jesus, pasting them together, and discarding the rest of the Gospels is a classic example of the rationalist approach. Jefferson did this twice, once while he was president (1803–4) and a second time (in 1819), in Greek, Latin, French, and English, after he retired from office.[6] He was confident he could distinguish between the "superstitions, fanaticisms, and fabrications" that came from the evangelists and Jesus' own "sublime ideas of the supreme being, aphorisms and precepts of the purest morality and benevolence," which "could not be the inventions of the grovelling authors who relate them."[7] Much was dispensable, simply because modern reason said it could not have happened that way. No attempt needed to be made to understand each evangelist on his own terms. "The difference is obvious to the eye and to the understanding...; he who, as I have done, will undertake to winnow this grain from it's [sic] chaff, will find it not to require a moment's decision. The parts fall asunder of themselves as would those of an image of metal and clay."[8]

Because the rationalists subordinate the authority of the Scriptures to the authority of contemporary reason and modern values, their position constitutes less a defense of biblical authority than a capitulation to the hesitations about it found in modern culture. Yet rationalism is an important indicator of the results of modern values; all the values of modern culture that I earlier outlined are endorsed by its religious outlook. And the rationalist position is important in quite another way, because it has become the archenemy of conservative Christians, who tend to read all subsequent developments as if they are but minor variations upon this approach. Many conservative Christians have labeled biblical interpreters rationalist whenever they have deviated from the conservative "party line," even when the interpreters have employed assumptions quite unlike those of true rationalists.[9]

When the rationalists criticize the Bible, their approach is very different from the discipline known as historical criticism. The rationalists winnow the sentences of the Bible in search of universal truths. The historical setting is unimportant except insofar as historical data can in some cases discredit the accuracy of particular passages. Discrepancies between different accounts of an incident provide grounds for distrusting both and for discrediting the Bible as a whole.[10] The presence of any description implying a suspension of natural laws, as natural laws are understood in modern times, or of any narrative departing from contemporary moral sensibilities also undermines the document's credibility. If in the present we do not observe natural laws to be miraculously suspended, then there must not have been any miracles, defined as interruptions of the causal order, in biblical times either. Reports of miracles must be explained away.

All this, of course, assumes an understanding of history as essentially unchanging. The perspectives and standards of today are assumed to be the perspectives and standards of yesterday. The narrative of one biblical author is to be judged by the same standards as another; no consideration is to be given to different historical circumstances. Discrepancies, therefore, are very significant.

This negative criticism constitutes the image of biblical criticism for conservatives who polemize against its dangers. Biblical criticism is interpreted as if it were a seamless robe. If negative criticism is destructive, then all criticism, of whatever variety, is thought to be destructive.[11] But a more developmentalist perspective has made possible a positive criticism — that is, a kind of criticism that can enhance the credibility of the Scriptures by explaining how discrepancies (e.g., between two or three different versions of an event) came about. Its objective is to defend the Scriptures over against the negative criticism of the rationalists and the antitradition bias of modern culture. Positive criticism has sought to understand the documents in their own context and to distinguish those features of each document that reflect the author's own purpose from those elements of the tradition with which the author was working. For the developmentalists the historical "rootedness" of the various biblical documents has confirmed their historical authenticity: the documents cannot be dismissed as pious frauds nor their redactors as groveling authors. They need to be understood on their own terms, and the value of what they have to say needs to be determined — initially at least — on the basis of internal, historical criteria rather than external, modern criteria. Whatever the accuracy of the books' contents, the books need to be taken seriously as historical documents.[12]

The exodus event can be used as a case study, first of all to illustrate the rationalist position and then, later, to illustrate each of the five other positions that I will discuss.

For the rationalist, the exodus event is of only marginal importance, because it happened to a particular group of people. God could not have revealed the divine self in any special way to this one group or provided them with insights or tasks in any way different from that of divine dealings with other peoples of the earth. By ascribing to this one event a pivotal and paradigmatic importance, the Bible unquestionably exaggerates its real significance. At best the historical story is but one illustration of a people deciding, in an appropriate response to natural and moral law, to achieve their own freedom from political tyranny. If God's assistance played a role, it did so only in the same degree that it would assist any other people in the course of a similar struggle.

On this view, the imagery of God's involvement has value only to show divine endorsement of such endeavors. God desires human freedom; enslavement is a transgression of the moral law. The story of the miraculous escape from Pharaoh's army is but the legendary embellishment of some fortuitous natural event. The details of the story contain enough discrepancies (e.g., God's telling the people to sit tight in one verse and to go forward in another; Exod. 13:13-15) to prevent us from determining what exactly did happen. What is significant is that the exodus sets the stage for the teaching of the Ten Commandments, that marvelous summary of the moral law which is so important to the rationalist.

The Supernaturalist Position

Supernaturalism operates within a static view of the past and bases the authority of the Bible on external miracles that interrupt the causal order.[13] Modern culture assumed a finite causal nexus. The supernaturalists begin with that same view of nature and, like the rationalists, picture the universe as a two-story house with a barrier between the supernatural and the natural. For the supernaturalists as well as the rationalists, miracles are defined as suspensions of the causal order in nature. A miracle is an occurrence for which no natural cause can be found and which hence has to be ascribed to a supernatural origin. Miracles are thus be definition extraordinary events, events that are objectively, noticeably different from other events in human experience.

All this and more the supernaturalist has in common with the rationalist, but they differ on one crucial point: the supernaturalist insists that miracles, as both the rationalist and the supernaturalist define them, have happened and continue to occur. Though a barrier exists between the natural and the supernatural, it is penetrated from time to time by God. God intervenes in the normal course of affairs; God breaks into the causal network.

Mechanism Thus supernaturalists accept the modern understanding of the world as a gigantic machine but modify that acceptance with an insistence that God continues to tinker with its operation, changing something here and stopping something there, all in order to assist human beings and make God known to them.

Autonomous reason Supernaturalism has some ambivalence toward the value of human autonomy and autonomous reason. On the one hand, it acknowledges in the main that modern culture operates according to its own standards, independent of religious authorization. It assumes that for human beings in general the operative criterion is reasonableness, and thus it seeks to convince by arguments and by appeals to objective evidence and expert opinion. But on the other hand, it seeks to place life—all of life, personal, social, and intellectual—back under the dominion of the Christian tradition. Though not an intended consequence, compartmentalized life may result in which the assumptions of contemporary culture hold sway in every area except the personal, which is placed under the guidance of principles grounded in the revealed will of God.

Progress and antitradition Although political and economic conditions may or may not improve, supernaturalism does not expect moral progress. It sees human beings as sinful and very much in need of special divine assistance. Apart from the revelation contained in the Scriptures there exists only moral and religious darkness. Saving insight and saving grace must be infused from outside the human situation. Thus the Scriptures become the repository of supernatural truth on the basis of which insight can be gained and blindness overcome. In the moral and religious sphere, at least, reason is not to be autonomous but should be subservient to revelation.

Objectivity and the infatuation with science Objectivity is both endorsed and rejected by supernaturalists. It is endorsed insofar as miracles are judged objectively valid and this is regarded to be important. It is endorsed insofar as religious truth is given the same status as scientific truth. But supernaturalism limits the scope of objectivity by expecting from the believer a special allegiance to revealed truths that is independent of rational scrutiny. Once arguments have been produced to convince a person that the testimony of the Bible should be accepted, then the rest of Christian doctrine is to be accepted as a package without further scrutiny. Reason is thought to offer no sound basis upon which to distinguish truth from falsehood in religious matters. Within the sphere of religion an appeal to an authority external to reason is necessary.

Supernaturalism also rejects objectivity in its recognition of special revelations to individuals and particular groups of people. The truth that is revealed is valid for everyone but is not a truth to be found on one's own without divine assistance. God's intervention is necessary, and such intervention is usually "specialized."

Optimism Supernaturalism does not hold human potential in high regard, since it takes the weight of sin and ignorance very seriously. In a curious, backhanded way, however, it still endorses human potential. With God's assistance, humans can understand revelation clearly. Revelation does not merely point to the truth, it embodies the truth, captures and contains it in words, in such a way as to inspire a great deal of confidence. Thus when theology says that God is unchanging, it means just that. No metaphor is involved; revelation points to no intractable reality that is somehow resistant to verbalization.

Individualism Though supernaturalism opposes the modern notion of autonomous individualism, the value reappears on another level. What it opposes is any sense that the individual can stand alone and critically appraise what is found in Christianity. Yet it places no emphasis on the corporate character of religious truth. Truth is, for it, sufficiently objective to be learned by individuals. The model is the individual scribe writing down the truth and the individual reader picking it up again from the text. Nowhere does it have to be refracted through a community in order to be deepened or corrected.

We have here a position that on the surface is openly opposed to modern culture but beneath the surface incorporates in differing ways several of its central values. Though often quite deliberately antimodernist, supernaturalism remains very much a modern position, forged in the crucible of the tension between Christianity and modern culture.

Supernaturalism attempts to defend the authority of the Bible over against the challenge of modern culture. Since theology immediately prior to modern culture assumed the authority of the Bible and since modern culture has questioned that assumption, supernaturalism tries to find arguments that at once appeal to modern values and go beyond them. The aim of supernaturalism is to buttress the crumbling foundations of premodern orthodoxy and, having shored up the foundations, to live in the same theological building, making the same theological assertions. In one sense nothing is new, but in another sense everything is new, because the assumptions, the context, and the intellectual framework are all different.

Supernaturalists operate with a static view of the world and its history. For them, cultural change affects peripherals only, and the essentials remain unchanged. But supernaturalists value historical information more highly than rationalists do. They prize the heritage of the church as the source of religious knowledge and do not wish to compromise its authority. Thus they have come to put a premium on historical accuracy. Historical accuracy is an objective matter. If a document from the past can be shown—or declared—to be objectively accurate, then its contents will have to be taken seriously by those imbued with modern culture. If taken seriously, this piece of the past will have been rehabilitated. Supernaturalism is trying to appeal to the criteria of modern culture in order to restore what modern culture has spurned: the Christian tradition. The historical accuracy of the Scriptures constitutes their major line of defense. "These we first prove authentic, historically credible, generally trustworthy, before we prove them inspired."[14]

In one example of how the supernaturalist argues, J. Gresham Machen in 1930 maintained that the virgin birth of Jesus was a historical fact. Toward the end of a long book amassing evidence to support his conclusion, he wrote,

> Here we have been interested merely in showing that the supernatural element is quite at the centre of these narratives, and that if the supernatural element is rejected the direct historical value of the narratives is gone. . . . As a natural phenomenon the virgin birth is unbelievable; only as a miracle, only when its profound meaning is recognized, can it be accepted as a fact. . . . It is only as such a stupendous miracle, only as a part of such a work of redemption, that the virgin birth of Christ can ever be accepted as a fact by reasonable men.
> But when it is so accepted, it is accepted, we must insist, as a *fact of history*.[15]

And again,

> The Biblical authors are not intending merely to give their readers inspiring poetry or an instructive

philosophy of religion; but they are intending to
narrate facts.... If, therefore, the virgin birth be
rejected, let us cease talking about the "authority of
the Bible" or the "infallibility of Scripture" or the
like. Let us rather say plainly that that authority and
the infallibility are gone.[16]

Machen's assumption is that historical accuracy is important and that
the value of Scripture in the modern world depends upon the historical
accuracy of its witness to the supernatural.

Modern culture itself, as it moved from the eighteenth to the
nineteenth century, came to value historical accuracy more and more.
The definition of the empirical and the rational was expanded to include
historical facts. Historical evidence counted. Supernaturalism mar-
shaled a defense of biblical authority on the basis of modern culture's
expanded definition of reliability. But it thereby departed significantly
from the theological tradition it sought to defend. That tradition had
distinguished the eternal from the temporal and had regarded the temporal as relatively unimportant. The eternal truths of revelation were
what mattered. Supernaturalism, for apologetic purposes, now placed
a stress on the temporal components of the Scriptures. Historical accuracy could establish their credibility. Ironically, supernaturalism's interest in temporal components was left behind as soon as the apologetic
task was done and dogmatics proper was resumed.

How then does supernaturalism defend the authority of the Bible?
There are two kinds of arguments: inductive and deductive. Its inductive arguments proceed by marshaling evidence in support of the accuracy and uniformity of the Scriptures, evidence that is not dependent
on Christian beliefs. A number of different inductive approaches have
been attempted. On one approach, ingenious harmonizations are
undertaken to explain away discrepancies alleged by the rationalists.[17]
On another approach there is an effort to locate extraordinary healings
and similar unexplained events in the present, as the empirical basis
for countering the argument: No miracles now, no miracles then, therefore unreliable reports. With this evidence the supernaturalist tries to
turn the argument around: Miracles are occurring right now, similar
miracles were possible back then, therefore the reports are plausible.

A third inductive approach defends the internal consistency of
the Scriptures by pointing to Old Testament passages that were quoted
by Jesus or cited and affirmed by New Testament authors. Old Testament prophecies are interpreted to be predictions, and detailed exam-
inations of the ways these predictions were fulfilled are conducted in

43

order to show the miraculous coherence of the entire biblical story. "If, therefore, the Old Testament reveals, hundreds of years in advance, what is coming to pass, omniscience must have directed the pen of the writer; i.e., these Scriptures, or at least their predictive parts, must be inspired."[18]

A fourth inductive approach draws data from archaeological discoveries and ancient Near Eastern history in order to support the accuracy of the scriptural accounts. At the end of an essay detailing recent archaeological discoveries pertaining to early Israelite history, for example, M. G. Kyle concludes, "The recent testimony of archaeology to Scripture, like all such testimony that has gone before, is definitely and uniformly favorable to the Scriptures at their face value, and not to the Scriptures as reconstructed by criticism."[19] Another author writing on the same theme observes, "It was pure ignorance, not superior knowledge, which led so many to discredit [biblical statements concerning the Hittites]. When shall we learn the inconclusiveness of negative testimony?"[20]

The structure of the inductive arguments is this: If the accounts of historical events found in the Bible are credible in every way, and those accounts include records of miracles, then miracles likely did occur. If miracles did occur, then the events reported have supernatural significance, because the occurrence of miracles is a sign of the supernatural at work in history. Miracles are the "alert signal" for the occurrence of revelation. The structure can be seen in the words of John H. Gerstner, as he lays out the steps in his argument for the authority of the Bible:

1. The Gospels, not assumed to be inspired, are generally recognized as highly reliable historical sources.
2. From these sources, even allowing for errors and discrepancies, the picture of a miracle-working Christ emerges.
3. Miracles can be performed only by God . . . .
4. Thus to use John Locke's expression, Christ's "credit as a proposer" of doctrine is established.
5. It is this Christ who teaches that he is the Son of God and that the Bible is the Word of God.[21]

Once established as the Word of God, of course, the Bible can be assumed to be totally accurate and its doctrinal authority will be guaranteed.

The second kind of argument is at bottom deductive—that is, logically dependent on Christian beliefs. Supernaturalism here begins with the traditional affirmation that the Bible is inspired, and draws the inference that since the Scriptures are inspired by God (i.e., since God has guided their authorship in such a way as to ensure their supernatural truth) and since God knows all and cannot err, the Scriptures must be without error. If the Bible is without error, then not only its theological content but also its historical data, and every other kind of assertion found in it, must be accurate. To claim, as the rationalists do, an ability to distinguish the true from the false according to the canons of contemporary reason is blasphemous. Instead, scriptural documents ought to be accepted as true in their totality.

In this deductive argument the Scriptures are themselves regarded as the product of a miracle, the miracle of inspiration, which breaks into the normal chain of historical events and pours supernatural content into the scriptural authors and documents. The Scriptures have an extraordinary origin, an extraordinary supernatural content, and an extraordinary historical accuracy. In the words of one exponent of the deductive approach, "We believe, teach, and confess that all Scripture is given by the inspiration of God the Holy Spirit and that God is therefore the true Author of every word of Scripture."[22] The same document continues, "*Since* the Holy Scriptures are the Word of God, they *contain no errors or contradictions* but are in all their parts and words the infallible truth."[23] On this argument, one does not need to demonstrate historically that the Bible is totally without errors or contradictions; inerrancy is an axiom that is brought to the Bible and governs its interpretation. The biblical books are therefore unique, unlike any other literature with which we come in contact. Their accuracy, in fact, not only holds for things occurring at the time of the books' composition but extends to references to things that came before (e.g., Genesis 1–11) and all that will follow (e.g., the timetable allegedly found in the Book of Revelation).[24]

Together, the inductive and deductive arguments are taken to support the credibility of the accounts as they stand in the Scriptures. They are taken to authorize mining the texts for their eternal as well as their historical truths. And when the texts are mined, post-Reformation (Zwinglian, Calvinist, Roman Catholic, Lutheran) orthodox theological teachings are rediscovered and traditional doctrines are reinforced. Because the view of the world is static and unchanging and because the truths affirmed are regarded to have a supernatural rather than a historical origin, it is believed that nothing needs to be changed. All can be reaffirmed, even if defended in a new way. The foundations of an old theology have been reinforced. The theological edifice appears to have been preserved, but innovation has occurred anyway. The authority of the Bible has been defended in ways not necessary and not even possible in a premodern world.

Supernaturalism pictures the exodus as very much a special event, an extraordinary intervention by God in the course of human history

45

to save the Israelites and reveal divine truth. The crossing of the Red Sea[25] is pictured much as it was in Cecil B. De Mille's film *The Ten Commandments*, with an objectively observable wall of water to the left and to the right. No mere east wind, no ordinary event this; it defies natural explanation. Discrepancies in the historical account are explained away. The authorship of Moses is affirmed. The event itself is regarded as significant, because the reader can be sure of God's involvement in any event so out of the ordinary. The implication is: Look here to find the supernatural truth. The Bible is important; it provides what cannot be found elsewhere.

The Evangelicalist Position

Evangelicalism operates with a static view of the past and bases the authority of the Bible on the experience of an "inner miracle" that circumvents the external grid of cause and effect.[26] Evangelicalists have less to say about the physical world "out there" than the supernaturalists do but, like supernaturalists and rationalists, are likely to accept the portrait of the natural world found in modern culture. They understand the physical universe to be a network of cause and effect, and they portray it as one large machine. For them a barrier separates the natural from the supernatural, and temporal change does not significantly affect an essentially static existence. These are all by now familiar notions, shared by modern culture, rationalism, supernaturalism, and evangelicalism.

The evangelicalists differ from rationalists and supernaturalists in their operative definition of a miracle. They consider a miracle to be an inner experience rather than an observed external event. Hence they restrict the barrier between the natural and the supernatural to physical matters. There is no barrier to direct action by the Holy Spirit on the inner person.

Evangelicalism assumes that reason operating alone would endorse the views of rationalism, but it claims that an inner experience of awakening gives individuals evidence for saying more than rationalists can say. The awakened person is convinced that special grace is available from God and that God is actively communicating it to individuals. The inner experience is a phenomenon of the individual's present, and therefore it is potentially credible to a modern culture that finds appeals to the past or to ecclesiastical authority suspect. The inner experience, as an experience, has to be taken seriously as a source of knowledge, according to the evangelicalist. And as an *inner* experience, it sidesteps the public inquiry associated with objective data. It cannot be disconfirmed by anyone else.

Autonomous reason   Evangelicalism does not challenge modern culture's estimate of autonomous reason but attempts to supplement it. Culture, it agrees, is not to be under the domination of religion; religion is not essentially a public matter. So, unlike supernaturalism, it does not seek to return society to direct religious control. The appropriate way to save society, according to evangelicalism, is to save the individuals in it. Persons who have been transformed by their inner experience will influence public life indirectly through their moral behavior and political wisdom.

Progress and antitradition   Thus evangelicalism does not challenge the value of progress but reposes confidence in the religious conversion of individuals, which it believes will improve society. Evangelicalism is ambivalent about modern culture's antagonism to tradition. On the one hand, evangelicalism defends Christianity against the bias of antitradition. It does so by validating Christian claims through appeal to an inner experience and then appropriating the tradition that agrees with that experience. The evangelicalists feel that every important aspect of the Christian tradition—doctrine, the Scriptures, worship patterns, and such—can be maintained. On the other hand, evangelicalism often foreshortens tradition through its insensitivity to historical distance. Frequently evangelicalists regard everything and everyone from the past as if they were contemporaries. They read the Bible without reference to the history of its interpretation and without reference to its historical setting. Moreover, they sometimes neglect the parts of the Christian tradition that do not seem substantiated experientially. Nonetheless, the overall effect of evangelicalism has been to reappropriate the Christian tradition and give it value in the face of modern culture.

Objectivity and the infatuation with science   Evangelicalism does not challenge the objectivity esteemed by modern culture, so long as this is taken as a value for science and the study of external things. But its cardinal belief is that inner experience has a strongly subjective cast and exists alongside that which can be investigated objectively.

Optimism   Evangelicalism gives qualified endorsement to the modern trust in human potential—qualified, because human sin needs to be acknowledged and redeemed. Yet it also gives a deeper endorsement, because the redeemed person is an individual with restored potential. Each person is free to exercise and develop the restored potential. For the redeemed, no societal impediments need to be addressed or conquered, and the road to holiness is open. Evangelicalists often endorse the possibility of "Christian perfection."

Individualism   Evangelicalism gives qualified assent also to the modern value of individualism. Its main qualification is that each individual needs to have a personal relationship with God in order to be whole. Its main endorsement of the value comes on the epistemological level, for no one is to trust another's experience. Only on the basis of one's own experience can one find Christianity credible. The Christian message does not meet people as a group but addresses individuals first, even if the individuals happen to be in the company of others. Fellowship is the result, not the presupposition, of conversion. The church is a voluntary association of persons who have had similar experiences. Though Christians are to live with close ties to others, evangelicalism employs largely individualistic categories to understand the Christian life on a theoretical or theological level.

Evangelicalism's argument for scriptural authority goes something like this: I have experienced an inner awakening, which has confirmed for me God's love. Because human beings have not changed in any essential way and God has not changed, persons in the past could have experienced the same thing I have. When I look at the Scriptures, I find that persons in biblical times (Samuel, Isaiah, the Samaritan woman at the well, Paul, Paul's hearers) did in fact experience personal awakening—indeed, that the Scriptures were written by and about awakened people. Their reports are similar enough to my own experience to be credible: the same Spirit must have been involved.

In this way the authority of the Bible is buttressed by personal experience, so that even in the face of modern culture Scripture must be taken seriously. The foundation of premodern theology having been shored up, evangelicalism is content to derive from the Bible essentially the same teachings one finds in post-Reformation orthodox theology. It endorses the same doctrines and cites the same scriptural passages as their basis. In a static world nothing needs to be revised, it can all be reaffirmed. As in supernaturalism, here too the appearance is conservative, the innovations are significant but camouflaged. The consequences of evangelicalism's appeal to inner experience are similar to those of the supernaturalist's appeal to objective external miracles. A new starting point supports a traditional post-Reformation theology against the bias of antitradition in modern culture.

But other consequences separate supernaturalism from evangelicalism. For one thing, evangelicalism avoids direct confrontation with modern culture. Given its beginning, it more easily compartmentalizes religion and society. Religion has to do with the inner and the subjective. Religious questions of the individual's relationship with God operate in a sphere easily distinguished from the outer, the public, the communal, the objective, the social, the political, and the cultural, where reason is allowed to hold sway. Reason need not be brought under the domination, and perhaps not even under the influence, of revelation. Supernaturalism tends toward confrontation, evangelicalism toward a softer accommodation with modern society.

Another difference between supernaturalism and evangelicalism springs from the way evangelicalism's emphasis on experience shifts the focus away from "true teachings." The list of important doctrines shortens as evangelicalists concentrate their attention on the soteriological matters most clearly associated with the experience of awakening. And the list, however short or long, is given a lesser importance, at least in comparison with supernaturalism. Supernaturalists draw their sustenance from a unified set of theological affirmations that they regard as more fundamental than any particular personal experience.

Evangelicalism pictures the exodus less as an extraordinary event than as the consequence of responding to the inner call. The exodus is the pilgrimage of those touched by God's Spirit, led by Moses, Miriam, and Aaron. Attention focuses on Moses and his response to God's call to lead the people forth, on Pharaoh and his refusal to heed God's call, and on the faith of the Israelites as they decide to follow, then waver, and then follow again. Evangelicalists feel no inclination to deny the reality of the outward miracle at the Red Sea, but they deem it less significant than what was happening inside the participants. Evangelicalism by itself does not force a decision between interpreting what really happened as a miraculous interruption of natural law and interpreting the east wind as a propitiously timed, otherwise quite natural occurrence.

Conservative Combinations

Supernaturalism and evangelicalism, though different in structure and though sometimes in conflict, hold positions regarding the Scriptures which are by no means incompatible. So-called conservative Protestants have often combined the two approaches, buttressing the authority of the Bible in two distinct but mutually reinforcing ways. This makes the dynamics of the conservative position by no means simple.

What enables the combination is that both the evangelicalist and the supernaturalist positions view history as static and accept the modern understanding of the causal nexus, and both consider post-Reformation theological formulations the correct exposition of Scripture. What also enables the combination is that each focuses on a different aspect of the tradition: evangelicalists on the inner and supernaturalists on the outer experiences of the people of God.

Though the two positions are often combined, they are sometimes found separately, and if combined, they are not always given equal weight. Conservatives in the Wesleyan, Methodist, and Baptist traditions lean toward evangelicalism; those in the Presbyterian, Lutheran, and Roman Catholic traditions are likely to draw consequences more closely allied with supernaturalism.

Supernaturalism regards historical criticism with hostility or, at best, suspicion. Whenever historical criticism endeavors to disentangle the pre-textual tradition, to identify diversity in the text, or to stress the interpretive latitude taken by the scriptural authors, it only, so far as the supernaturalist is concerned, undermines the reliability of the authors as objective witnesses. Thus supernaturalism regards almost all historical criticism as negative criticism. Evangelicalism, by contrast, regards historical criticism with either indifference or a somewhat milder suspicion. It is a matter of indifference to the degree that it focuses on what did or did not happen externally, because the important developments were internal anyway. Historical criticism is viewed with suspicion, however, to the degree that it emphasizes the temporal and cultural distance between the text and the contemporary reader. Such distance is inimical to the reader's confidence that persons in biblical times had the same experience as the contemporary who has been awakened.

In this chapter, three positions have been examined, all of which employ an understanding of history as static and unchanging. The first abandons the independent authority of the Bible; it makes no claim that is not confirmed by contemporary reason. The second and the third follow different paths to the goal of reasserting the authority of the Bible. They appeal to one or another of the canons of modern culture. Having defended the authority of the Bible, each is content to draw from it a set of traditional, post-Reformation theological teachings. As theories of authority, supernaturalism and evangelicalism select certain features of modern culture with which to link certain features of the biblical materials. Neither is exclusively biblical. Both involve extrabiblical appeals. As theories of authority, both positions appeal to history— either to a person's personal subjective history or to the "objective" accounts of the past provided by written records. The assumption is that history is sufficiently empirical to count, to be credible according to the canons of modern culture. In this assumption both theories are distinctively modern.

3

Responses within a Dynamic World View

The portraits of God in supernaturalism and evangelicalism share one feature: God is separated from the natural order by a barrier that must be penetrated or circumvented. The finite and the infinite are considered to be distinct. In contrast, ecclesial developmentalism and analogical developmentalism affirm far more harmony between the infinite and the finite, a harmony restored by the incarnation. Either the opposition between the finite and the infinite has actually been overcome by the incarnation, or the incarnation has shown that the finite and the infinite have been wrongly opposed and incorrectly understood. In Jesus the Christ and in the history of the church the human and the divine have been reunited. The unification is one of communion or harmony, not of identification or an obliteration of differences between God and human beings. God and creation cooperate, work in complementary ways, and coalesce in events of disclosure.

Both ecclesial developmentalism and analogical developmentalism need to reformulate received teachings about God and the human. They need to challenge some assumptions of modern culture as well as some of the old theological understandings. They must reembody Christian teachings in new categories and Concepts. In this regard both positions are unlike supernaturalism and evangelicalism, which start anew but in the end endorse post-Reformation orthodox theological teachings.

The two positions differ from evangelicalism and supernaturalism in still another important way. They operate with a developmentalist understanding of the past, which sees in history organic change and growth. The main advantage of this understanding is to rehabilitate the past and counteract modern culture's tendency to dismiss its cultural inheritance in favor of current knowledge and human hopes concerning the future. A developmentalist viewpoint will not dismiss a document from the past simply because it deviates from current attitudes and understandings. What is more, it will try to understand and explain the discrepancies between documents emerging from different settings. It will see the past as important, at least as an extended prelude to the present. The past can help a person understand the shape of present culture and society and in this way be a valuable source of information and insight.

Developmentalism, because of its organic imagery of growth and development, perceives the negative biblical criticism of the rationalists to be anachronistic. The rationalists' biblical criticism employs assumptions familiar to the modern world but alien to the times in which the books of the Bible were written and collected. Both the ecclesial and the analogical developmentalists find it important to pay close attention to cultural change through time. And because of their understanding of the way God works in history, they find cultural conditioning to be an important component of the biblical documents. God, for them, works through human beings, and the resulting texts bear the marks of human finitude as well as of divine inspiration.

Whereas supernaturalism judges there to be a static, unchanging content to the Christian tradition, ecclesial developmentalism and analogical developmentalism hold Christian thought to be dynamic, changing, and growing. That accounts, they think, for the "primitive" character of some biblical perceptions—for example, in the area of natural science. And because different documents occupy different places in the evolutionary development of Christian doctrine, discrepancies are not automatically prejudicial to the documents' historicity or their value. They expect new procedures for interpreting history to counteract negative criticism, and the credibility of historical documents to be reestablished with the help of quite different assumptions about their role.

It is important to notice that ecclesial and analogical developmentalism are not borrowing their developmentalist understanding of history from modern culture. Instead, they have created it. Fifty to sixty years before Darwin's *On the Origin of Species*, Christian theologians were pioneering evolutionary models to understand the church. During the first half of the nineteenth century the most freguent test case for historical methodology was early Christianity, including the documents that now make up the New Testament. Christian attempts to understand Christian origins more precisely and to appropriate them more carefully led to the developmentalist understanding of history. Though theological thinkers employing developmentalist categories have often been called modernists by conservative rhetoric, the label of modernist is incorrect, since it implies an endorsement of modern culture. Developmentalists do not endorse but challenge modern culture, and they defend the value of the Christian tradition, including the Scriptures, by employing assumptions and categories different from those that modern culture and evangelicalist and supernaturalist conservatism share.

Against a modern denial of tradition, developmentalists try to amend the modern notion of tradition to take into account how tradition develops, whereas conservatives work within the notion of tradition that modern culture espouses.

It is also important to notice that, just as supernaturalism and evangelicalism are not incompatible, so ecclesial and analogical developmentalism can fit together. Persons who hold a moderate or liberal or historical-critical view of the Bible often combine aspects of both in their approach. Ecclesial and analogical developmentalism each find a positive role for historical criticism; they use it to illumine the historical rootedness of the biblical documents and thereby to undergird the documents' credibility as sources for understanding Christianity. According to both positions, historical criticism also illumines the process of composition and canonization, and consequently can disclose the central purpose of each document. That central purpose is what can be appropriated by later generations for whom other matters are now irrelevant. In sum, historical criticism both demonstrates the credibility of the documents as products of the past and assists in bridging the distance between the documents and the present.

The external (i.e., what happens "out there" in the world) receives relatively greater emphasis in supernaturalism, whereas the internal (i.e., what happens "in here," within the person of faith) is given greater emphasis in evangelicalism. A similar difference separates ecclesial from analogical developmentalism. Ecclesial developmentalism places a relatively greater emphasis on the internal life of the community of faith. For it, doctrines are expressions of the consciousness or faith of the church. Analogical developmentalism places a relatively greater emphasis on the external, on what is true about the world and God. For supernaturalism and analogical developmentalism the thoughts of the individual should in some way be conformed to the given, even if that given is understood differently in each case. Thus, though the gulf separating the two nondevelopmentalist from the two developmentalist positions is greater than any similarities they share, supernaturalism is in some way similar to analogical developmentalism and evangelicalism is in some way similar to ecclesial developmentalism.

The Ecclesial Developmentalist Position

Ecclesial developmentalism, operating within a developmentalist view of the past, bases the authority of the Bible on an appeal to the historical continuity of the Christian community and the role played by the biblical documents in that history.[1] The ecclesial position begins with dissatisfaction concerning the rationalist understanding of religion, which seems to impoverish Christianity by denying its uniqueness. Ecclesial developmentalism therefore attempts to recapture the elements of Christianity tied to its uniqueness, namely, the role and status of Jesus the Christ and the authority of the Scriptures as a channel of special revelation. In order to defend the uniqueness of Christianity it needs to argue, against rationalism and modern culture, that the past—at least that part of it making up the Christian heritage—matters.

Ecclesial developmentalism rejects the dichotomy between the natural and the supernatural which is operative in all three of the positions that view the past as static. It assumes that everything that happens in history is capable of having simultaneously a human and a divine cause. Thus a miracle is no longer a suspension or a circumvention of the causal order, it is instead an event in which God's presence and participation are disclosed. A miracle is at once a product of finite causes and an instrument of God's purpose. As a result, there may be no objective, observable differences between a miraculous and a nonmiraculous event. God may be present in both, but in the miracle God's involvement is disclosed and noticed. The distinguishing feature lies in what is perceived by the observer.

God's influence effects incremental changes in human history. The most significant incremental changes are "relative miracles," that is, events in which new, even startling advances occur through a combination of divine and human or natural causality. Relative miracles helped bring Christianity into being, and they have propelled its evolution. God does not work—at least not usually—through the absolute miracles that are pivotal for supernaturalism, wherein the natural order is broken into and revelation is given in once-for-all completeness. God works through incremental change.

The developmentalist notion of history makes possible such an understanding of God's role. Were history static, were things essentially unchanging, relative miracles would involve God only in the peripheral, the transitory, the nonessential. But once a developmentalist model of history is accepted, God can be understood to effect significant, genuine changes without having to arrest the natural sequence of human developments. Relative miracles can produce important changes.

The notion of a relative miracle and of incremental change causes considerable consternation to the supernaturalist, who poses an either/or: either an event has a human or natural cause or it has a supernatural cause. When ecclesial developmentalists argue for joint causation, the supernaturalist accuses them of eliminating the divine in favor of a humanism or a naturalism or an "immanentalism."[2]

The reason for calling this position *ecclesial* developmentalism is that it regards the concrete historical community, the church, to be the temporal and human link between Jesus and us. In the absence of absolute miracles, the influence of Jesus cannot reach us except through a linkage that is human as well as divine. The Spirit does not leap over historical continuities but rather works through them. God works along with human beings and human traditions to bring us into contact with the Son. The church is the channel of the Spirit's work.

The ecclesial position emphasizes the continuity and the periodic revitalization of the history of God's people, a story going back to and antedating Jesus. The Bible is a collection of books representing the earliest stages of that history. Each document can be located and understood in terms of its unique place in and its unique contribution to that history. Without those books, we would be left uncertain about the very important lines of historical continuity that join us to Jesus, the prophets, the exodus, and the patriarchs. Not only are scriptural figures and events rooted in the history of God's people, not only do they represent and reflect the earliest stages of the community of faith, but they also form and shape the contemporary community and thereby ensure the continuity of its ongoing, evolving identity.

The Bible is valuable for those inside the community of faith because it illuminates the self-understanding of the community. It keeps members of the community in contact with their origins and, in that way, with God's activity in and through their origins. The Bible is credible in a somewhat different way to those outside the community. Each document makes sense by reference to its unique historical location and therefore cannot be dismissed as unreliable, even by outsiders. The biblical documents are similarly tied to the self-identity of a present community and therefore are important for understanding contemporary culture. Because the Bible is tied to a specific community rather than being an extraordinary, supernaturally produced, universally applicable document, it lays no direct burdens on those outside the community. They can acknowledge its historical credibility without the existential consequence of obedience to its injunctions. The outsider may say that the Bible is others' book, important to the Christian church, and can respect its importance without coming to faith or joining the community. The ecclesial position is therefore similar to the evangelicalist in that the authority of the Bible is explicitly tied to those who have faith.

In response to the challenge of modern culture, the ecclesial view says that we must look to the past, because only by examining the past can we perceive the incremental process through which God has revealed the divine self. Encounters with God in the present are without specific content unless informed by an understanding of the larger revelatory process and by the larger perspective such an understanding affords. Christians look back to the Scriptures not to find something universal and objective but to discover something specific about the Christian view of God and the development of their religious community.

Objectivity and the infatuation with science Ecclesial developmentalism thus rejects the demand in modern culture that objective, universal reason ascertain what is true. Every claim to religious truth is seen to be inherently conditioned by the peculiarities of historical circumstances. Religious communities are inherently diverse, and their unique histories condition their claims to religious truth. No common teachings can be found except by the most arbitrary methods of selection and extraction. Whatever the value of objectivity and universality elsewhere, those values are not appropriate to revelation. Religious statements are never detached but are always embedded in the perspectives of the persons or groups making the statements. In religion there are only better or worse, more or less adequate statements, and a certain amount of diversity is inevitable.

Autonomous reason The ecclesial view allows modern culture to have its autonomy but rejects its claims to hegemony. The criteria that modern culture requires scientific inquiries to meet cannot be applied to Christianity without violating the dynamic center of that religion. Human existence is diverse enough that religion must be understood on its own terms. It cannot be reduced to knowledge and morals. The rules that govern in nature and in science cannot be applied, without qualification, to religion.

Progress and antitradition The ecclesial position neither endorses nor denies modern culture's belief in progress. It does, however, find corporate sin to be a problem that needs to be overcome. Thus it is somewhat less optimistic about the promise of education and somewhat less convinced of the individual's capacity for moral self-improvement than rationalism and modern culture are. Behind its reservations stand its focus on the community rather than the individual and its inherently social understanding of human beings.

Individualism It is not surprising therefore that ecclesial developmentalism does not exalt the autonomous individual. The identity of individuals is formed and shaped by social contacts. Outside Christianity, social contacts are often—and in the most fundamental sense, inescapably—deleterious. Within Christianity, the influence of Jesus, as communicated through other members of the community and the activity of the Spirit, is redemptive. In either case the focus is communal.

Optimism   Ecclesial developmentalism has a higher view of human potential than supernaturalism does, because for it human beings participate in God's revelation and redeeming activity. No intervention by a purely supernatural agency is necessary or desirable. The ecclesial view of human potential is lower, however, than that of rationalism or modern culture, because, according to it, humans are not really free to reorient their lives without the assistance, the influence, and the redemptive grace of God. Human potential is theoretically very great but in actuality severely limited.

Mechanism   Ecclesial developmentalism does not accept the mechanical model of the universe favored by modern culture. For it, the universe is under divine and human influence simultaneously. The universe is spirit and nature, it is subjective and objective, and to portray it as a machine is to oversimplify to the point of distortion.[3]

Because the ecclesial view ties different parts of the Scriptures to different points in the organic growth of the church, diversity within the Scriptures ceases to be a problem. It merely furnishes clues to the location of the texts in the history of God's people. To demonstrate the historical credibility of the Bible it is not necessary to show its internal harmony, as supernaturalism believes. It is enough to tie each diverse element of the texts to a distinguishable point in history. Diversity is simply a reflection of the way God works through human particularities.

Ecclesial developmentalism does not stress the direct doctrinal significance of the words of Scripture. Rather it finds the words expressive of the church's awareness of God in Christ. The words are primarily poetic, rhetorical, and liturgical, and only secondarily didactic.[4] The teachings of the church need to be formulated anew by every generation in order to reflect changes in faith. The ecclesial position's receptivity to, and encouragement of, reformulation leads to considerable divergence from supernaturalism and evangelicalism, which continue to affirm an older, post-Reformation theology and its interpretation of the Bible. Post-Reformation theology, formulated in a different historical setting, regarded the Scriptures primarily as the textbook for correct doctrinal teachings. For ecclesial developmentalism, on the other hand, the Scriptures do not contain doctrines so much as they witness to and shape the consciousness of the church, which is then expressed in doctrines. The net result is a revised theology, one using a vocabulary oriented toward the dynamics of a community experiencing growth and development: and oriented toward an understanding of divine-human relationships predicated on proximity and compatibility. The barrier between the divine and the human has been overturned—a barrier erected by modern culture and acceded to by rationalism, supernaturalism, and evangelicalism alike.

In comparison with the old theology of supernaturalism and evangelicalism, the ecclesial position's theology seems more modest— indeed, even timid in its claims. It projects itself only as representing the consciousness of the church, not as having uncovered a series of unchanging, supernaturally authenticated ontological truths. On the other hand, in comparison with the theology found in rationalism, it seems boldly expansive, restoring the uniqueness of Christianity and reappropriating the Christian tradition as determinative of present Christian identity.

On this approach the most important thing about the exodus is its impact on the people who experience it. Attention focuses on their consciousness of the world, themselves, and God, and how this comes from defining the significance of the event and appropriating its impact. What happens in the exodus is likely a relative miracle: the agency of God combines with the otherwise natural phenomenon of the east wind blowing back the marshy waters. What happens is a relative miracle of liberation in which the agency of God combines with the natural leadership of Moses and Aaron and the desire of the slaves in Egypt for freedom. Most important, Israel perceives in the exodus the hand of God; the event thus becomes formative in Israel's endeavors to express its own theology.

The Analogical Developmentalist Position

Analogical developmentalism, employing a developmentalist understanding of the past, bases the authority of the Bible on the similarity between the biblical message and the way things happen in the world as a whole. There are some similarities between analogical developmentalism and ecclesial developmentalism. Not only do the two positions share a developmentalist understanding of history but both also emphasize the coming together of the divine and the human in ordinary events that, when properly perceived, can be revelatory of God. For both, Jesus the Christ has overcome the barrier—or revealed the absence of a barrier—between the natural and the supernatural. In Hegel's words, "The result is that we must emancipate ourselves from the bogey of the antithesis between finite and infinite."[6]

David Griffin, for instance, sees God's influence to lie in persuading: God "lures" human beings toward creative advances. "In terms of this conceptuality," he remarks, "there is no antithesis between divine influence and creaturely self-determination."[7] On Griffin's view,

> no event would be conceived as simply or wholly an
> act of God. For the theologian would think in terms

of each event as having a multiplicity of antecedent causes upon it, and also of it having some degree of self-determination, even in relation to God's initial aims.[8]

In seeking God, it is not necessary to chase after the extraordinary. God's influence is potentially—potentially, since God's lure may be rejected— a factor in every event.

Like the ecclesial view, analogical developmentalism emphasizes the importance of Jesus the Christ—of Jesus not just as a teacher but as the incarnate Son of God. In one way or another the Christ-event is believed to reveal the characteristic activity of God in relationship to the world and human beings. Analogical developmentalism is, however, somewhat less interested than ecclesial developmentalism in the uniqueness of Christianity. Not content to analyze the role of the Christ in and for the church, it seeks to emphasize the universal truth of what has been revealed and communicated through the symbols, stories, and teachings of religion.

The major difference between the ecclesial and analogical positions is that in analogical developmentalism the emphasis shifts from the concrete historical community to the cosmological truth of Christianity.[9] Attention falls more heavily on ideational content than on human experience, though the ideational content is understood in the most dynamic of terms. Christianity has, according to analogical developmentalism, given us a true portrait of the way things work in the world. The position is called *analogical* developmentalism because its grounds for holding the Bible true are that the developmental process that Scripture reveals is analogous to the developmental process that can be discerned in the world, and vice versa. It is true that little correlation exists between the biblical view and the outlook of modern culture, but a deeper, more adequate philosophy can be constructed. The endeavor to fashion philosophical systems that at once capture cosmological reality and reflect Christian truth is evident in Hegel's thought and in Whitehead's process philosophy. The analogical position could thus be called *philosophical* or *cosmological* developmentalism, because the appeal is really to philosophical insight into the nature of reality. As Hegel asserts, the Bible in particular and Christianity in general reveal in symbolic or pictorial form the same insights that a true philosophy expresses in more abstract form.

Another difference between the ecclesial and the analogical positions is that analogical developmentalism often portrays God as affected by the process of development and change. The idea is that God is influenced by occurrences in the world. God experiences natural and human events as painful or joyous or the source of increased awareness. According to William Beardslee, for example,

> the Old Testament and the New develop a picture of the struggle between God and man which sees God as so deeply involved in the struggle that he cannot remain the remote and unchanging God of archaic religion. God is concerned for the *new* outcome, not just for a repetition of the original situation. A further deepening of this perspective... transforms the struggle to see God as the persuader rather than as the one who compels. Even more: he suffers with and in the world.[10]

Analogical developmentalism affirms tradition over against modern culture, because from tradition we derive our sense of how things fit together. Our present experience provides only a tiny glimpse of the whole. Indeed, even if we were to understand everything occurring in the present, we would see only a tiny slice of the temporal scope of things. Thus, in order to catch some vision of the whole of reality, we must both understand the past and understand the present in terms of the past. Tradition does not have the kind of authority that limits or binds persons, but it produces understanding that informs our actions in the present and future. It sets us free from bondage to too narrow an understanding of ourselves and reality.

The Scriptures are thus credible because they are part of tradition, because they record the dynamics of God's involvement in the world, and because they are true.[11] They are true not in the sense of recording accurate bits of information but in the sense of indicating the nature of reality and the character of God's involvement in the world.[12] The ultimate test of the credibility of the Scriptures is thus how well the biblical contents correlate with reality as a whole, understood dynamically and developmentally. Historical criticism is valuable because it uncovers the dynamic, developmental character of the ideas found in the Scriptures. It shows how the traditions came into being and how they have been reinterpreted to keep up with the movement of God and God's people.

Autonomous reason Analogical developmentalism does not share modern culture's enthusiasm for cultural autonomy beholden only to reason. To the degree that culture strives for autonomy, it cuts itself off from a broader vision of what has been and what can be. Religion is an integral part of any vision of the whole, and because Christianity, properly understood, is a source of insight, it must be allowed to contribute to our total vision.

Analogical developmentalism holds reason in high regard, but only when it is understood dynamically. For it believes that the ahistorical criteria of rationalism are too narrow. It also believes that symbols are important. They nourish reason by enticing reason forward beyond its previous boundaries. They are not merely expressive, as the ecclesial view suggests, but they also disclose something of truth about the universe, even beyond the religious community. Rationalism was seriously wrong when it disparaged as superstitious everything not measuring up to the standards of static reason.

Progress and antitradition   Progress is possible, on the analogical view, but progress never leaves tradition behind. Tradition may be transformed, but it is inevitably carried along into the next state. Education may facilitate progress, but if so, it must be a more complete education than that envisioned in modern culture. Science and morality are not enough; they must be enriched by the wisdom gained from a wider vision of human development.

Objectivity and the infatuation with science   Analogical developmentalism regards objectivity as a worthwhile but inadequate goal. In itself, it is superficial. The underlying dynamics of an event or an idea are more important than the concrete data. The impact of the event and its interpretation are part of its reality. Thus in order really to advance understanding or to contribute to human progress, objective knowledge needs to be taken up into a higher vision of the whole.

Optimism   Human beings, on the analogical view, have potential, but not as much as rationalism and modern culture postulate. We never completely escape our place in the overall development of things. We may influence the overall development as well as be influenced by it, but we never act completely outside it. Our decisions are constrained by a limited set of concrete options. We are called not only to realize ourselves but to participate in what is true and right, which is always corporate and always temporally conditioned.

Individualism   Thus, for analogical developmentalism, human beings are not autonomous individuals but are inherently social. They inherit the past and influence the whole in either a creative or a destructive way. They are never isolated. Indeed, not just are human beings tied together, but God and nature are tied with human beings as well, so that any action influences the well-being of all.

Mechanism   Analogical developmentalism consequently denies the adequacy of a mechanical view of the universe, for the universe includes God, human beings, and nature in process through time. The universe is spirit and nature, divine and human, subjective and objective. To portray it as a machine is to distort its character.

61

What analogical developmentalism values most highly in the Scriptures are the symbols, images, and stories that are translatable into dynamic ideas. Like supernaturalism, it reads the Scriptures essentially as a source of didactic content, though in its case of content understood dynamically. In the Scriptures we learn the truth about God, the world, and ourselves. And the history of Christianity, indeed the history of the world, can be written as the history of dynamic ideas embodied in various ways by concrete communities and individuals. For analogical developmentalism, our lives are expressions of the ideas that govern them. This contrasts with ecclesial developmentalism, for which ideas are considered merely expressive of our life in community.

The analogical position leads to the conclusion that post-Reformation orthodox theology, which was formulated within the framework of static concepts, needs to be reformulated in more dynamic terms, with attention to issues that it did not explicitly discuss. Attention must be paid to the doctrine of God (which it largely assumed), to the relationship between human beings and creation, to the role of the church in the world, and to a host of issues outside the rather narrowly soteriological focus of post-Reformation theology. Reformulation is needed not in order to repudiate the past but in order to reappropriate our heritage in a more contemporary form, indeed, in order to reappropriate the whole of the Christian tradition in ways that bring it into dialog, though not necessarily agreement, with the whole of contemporary learning.

On the analogical view, the importance of the exodus is the process it reveals and embodies—the process of liberation from bondage. Because God is involved along with human beings, the exodus discloses something of God's character. To resist liberation is to oppose God and the direction of human history. To engage in exploitation is not only to harm others but also to bring pain to God. By understanding the exodus we can understand reality—the whole fabric of political, social, economic, and cultural events—and our role in reality. In the matter of what really happens in the exodus, analogical developmentalism will probably also affirm the relative miracle of a timely east wind. But its focus is away from what really happens, from the events within the concrete historical community of Israel in flight from Pharaoh, and on the implications of the exodus for perceptions of reality in this or any age. For the analogical view it is only as the particular is tied to a vision of the whole that it takes on genuine importance.

The Dynamic Humanist Position

Dynamic humanism operates with a developmentalist view of the past but undercuts the authority of the Bible by appealing to a process of human development that occurs independent of Christianity.[13] It sees human history to be moving away from Christianity toward a more general humanism. Thus, it does not underline the importance of the Christian heritage except insofar as Christianity has carried humanity toward humanism. It considers most of the distinctive Christian themes obsolete, and certainly dispensable wherever humanism has been attained. For it the propelling dynamic of historical development has been not God but social developments and human aspirations.

Autonomous reason On the dynamic humanist view, culture is once more viewed as autonomous, as proceeding best without any sense of transcendence, without any encumbrance by Christianity. On this view, reason is judged an adequate basis on which to proceed. To be sure, reason is understood in a more dynamic and historical way than it is in rationalism, and symbols may be regarded more positively than they are in rationalism. But human wisdom remains the ultimate authority.

Progress and antitradition Dynamic humanism endorses modern culture's belief in progress and denies religious tradition any ongoing contemporary significance apart, in some cases, from helping to tutor the uneducated in the direction of progress.

Objectivity and the infatuation with science Dynamic humanism regards objectivity with mixed feelings. On the one hand, it accepts objectivity and universality as criteria of truth. But on the other hand, it nourishes ideals and aspirations itself for which there is no empirical basis. By trusting its aspirations it hopes to see them more and more fully embodied.

Optimism According to dynamic humanism, human potential is unlimited. Even attributes traditionally ascribed to God can be legitimate goals for humanity as a whole. Not individuals but humanity as a whole can be all-powerful, all-knowing, and so on.

Individualism Dynamic humanism does not view the individual as autonomous. Human beings are for it inherently social, just as they are for ecclesial and analogical developmentalism. Individuals are enmeshed in the larger community in such a way that they benefit from the progress of the whole. Accordingly, they should work for the good of the whole. Selfishness is to be transcended. Dynamic humanism is frequently found in the company of a high degree of ethical sensitivity and moral behavior.

Mechanism In some cases dynamic humanism endorses the mechanical model of the universe, merely qualifying it with a linkage to the human spirit. In other cases it attempts a rival cosmology that is more organic and vitalistic.

Dynamic humanism undercuts the authority of the Bible, not so much because the Bible is full of contradictions or contains historical inaccuracies or fails to recognize natural law as because it is the product of a bygone era. Its day is past. It was valid once upon a time, but progress has now overtaken it. But even rationalism finds ethical insights of some ongoing value in Scripture. Similarly dynamic humanism finds ethical insights there, though mostly with a focus on the social instead of the individual, on the contextual rather than the ontological. The remainder of the Bible has little claim on us, it thinks, unless reinterpreted along humanist lines. Scripture may help us envision the future by holding up humane ideals, but in this it merely stands alongside other visionary literature, whether religious or utopian in a nonreligious style. Dynamic humanism thus appreciates the Bible not for its uniqueness but precisely for what it shares with other literature. The universally human—in the sense of what can be—is for it the criterion for selecting and ascribing lasting value to certain elements of the Scriptures.

The exodus is portrayed by dynamic humanism as an escape from bondage, an exercise in human growth as the chains holding a whole people are shattered and the people moves on in the joy and anxiety of freedom. There is no involvement of the divine. The east wind is a fortunate coincidence, but the resolve of the people to go forward is what makes the difference. The interpretation Scripture gives this event is a primitive religious ascription to God of what really should be ascribed to human beings. The celebration ought to read, "We did it," not, "God saved us."

In dynamic humanism there is a genuinely symbolic interpretation of the Scriptures. Talk about God symbolizes human endeavors and human hopes. The interpretations of Scripture offered in ecclesial and analogical developmentalism are not, properly speaking, symbolic. They are as literal as the interpretations offered in supernaturalism and evangelicalism. But *literal* means different things for texts of different natures, and the nature of scriptural texts is what is at issue between the positions. Characterizations of conservative exegesis as literal and developmentalist exegesis as symbolic are inaccurate and unhelpful. To interpret a poetic passage of the Bible as if it were an eyewitness account aiming at scientific objectivity is not to interpret it literally. To acknowledge the symbolic character of Revelation is not to interpret is symbolically: one is merely paying attention to the character of the text as it stands. The developmentalists are as interested in the historical meaning of biblical texts as the supernaturalists are. Though they are ready to delve behind the text through a critical analysis of its features, they are as interested in being literal as the conservatives are.

To interpret Genesis 1 with a view to penetrating to what it said to its original readers is to take it no less literally, surely, than to interpret it as a record of geological history.

Comparison

I have included rationalism and dynamic humanism in the discussion in order to show that neither a static nor a developmentalist understanding of history is intrinsically dangerous or intrinsically safe. Either can be used as a framework for undermining the authority of the Bible or for reinforcing its authority over against modern culture.

The four remaining positions all affirm the value of tradition over against modern culture. Supernaturalism, evangelicalism, ecclesial developmentalism, and analogical developmentalism all affirm the authority of the Bible, in the sense of maintaining that it offers something indispensable for Christians above and beyond contemporary ideas and values. All four positions endorse some values found in modern culture and reject others. All four attempt to explain and defend the Scriptures by appealing to certain assumptions inherent in modern culture without endorsing the full range of modern values. That is, each position is a theory of biblical authority that brings selected features of modern culture into relationship with selected features of the Bible. None of the theories confines its attention to affirmations found in the Bible; each involves extrabiblical appeals.

All four of the positions appeal to history as the touchstone for the credibility of the Scriptures. Supernaturalism finds in the Bible objectively accurate accounts of the past. Evangelicalism bases biblical authority on an inner personal history. Ecclesial developmentalism finds reassurance in the historicity of the biblical documents, each locatable in a particular time and place. Analogical developmentalism finds in the Bible a correspondence to the whole dynamic history of the world which can be known philosophically. Though these are four quite different kinds of appeals, each position has referred in one way or another to history in developing its unique response to the challenge of modern culture.

In response to the mechanistic view of the world found in modern culture, each of the four positions employs a different image of God's relation to the world and emphasizes different aspects of the biblical narratives. Each image has extrabiblical components. The supernaturalist notion of miracle is not "more biblical" than the developmentalist notion of relative miracle, nor is the developmentalist understanding of miracle more biblical than the evangelicalist, because all the understandings assume a view of the world not found in the Bible itself. A static view of history, if properly nuanced, is not any less—or more— biblical than a developmentalist view. Nor does the Bible uniformly support or reject a notion of God as affected by the world to the degree of being subject to change. To adjudge as unbiblical the notion that the world can cause changes in God, one has to ignore the biblical descriptions of God as repenting (i.e., as undergoing a change of mind) and as agonizing over Israel's rebellion.

On any of these issues the adoption of one position rather than another remains a theological judgment rather than a logical deduction from uniform biblical evidence. The decision to accept any one of the positions in turn influences how the Bible is read and understood. Some passages of the Bible will fit one position better than another, but often this will not be noticed. For the assumptions articulated in a theory condition what the reader expects to find in the Bible. Thus, one's own views may seem more in harmony with the Bible than others', but that impression is at root illusory. Many different images are capable of conveying the gospel, but because they are extrabiblical, they are not themselves part of the gospel.

If an image is within the range of possibilities given by Christian identity, then the decision to favor it over another must be based on reasons apart from biblicalness. Each of the four tradition-affirming positions regarding biblical authority has validity for particular sets of concerns and for particular settings. It is important to take into account the day-to-day outlook of the persons in the Christian community who are studying and appropriating the biblical message. If they routinely work with a static view of the world, there is little Christian reason to require that they adopt a developmentalist view of it in order to understand the gospel. Contrariwise, if they in general employ a dynamic, developmentalist view of the world, there is little reason to require that they think of it as essentially static and unchanging in order to understand the gospel. There is no need to place stumbling blocks on the way to the gospel.

In life outside the sanctuary more and more of the people in our society view the world in developmentalist terms. Evolutionary models influence their understanding of animal life, human culture, geology, and the like. This is one reason to choose a developmentalist image of God's relation to the world. But only when a particular image of God's relation to the world has been confused with the gospel itself is it of benefit deliberately to confront someone with a different one. Understanding an alternative can help people refine their understanding of the gospel and increase their sensitivity to fellow Christians who employ other images. In that case, understanding an alternative is a step toward Christian maturity.

The gospel can be communicated by and to persons who hold any one of the four positions. In order for a Bible to be edifying, it is not necessary to insist that everyone in the study group adopt the same view of biblical authority. Whenever one of the positions claims to represent *the* biblical approach to a topic, it is overlooking its own extra-biblical appeals.

Moreover, all four positions are modern, in the sense that they are formulated in response to the challenges of modern culture. None is *the* traditional theory. All are contextual. All are dated. As modern culture recedes from the scene, all four positions lose their impact. Other theories will need to be formulated to explain the authority of the Bible to a postmodern world, and new tensions will need to be addressed.

If each of the four positions employs its own imagery for God's relation to the world, each also understands revelation differently. Supernaturalism sees in revelation the communication of correct information about God and things "upstairs"; it fully expects such information to be stated adequately in propositional form. Evangelicalism expects a love message focused on the individual and communicated in such a way as to elicit a personal response. Ecclesial developmentalism understands revelation to be a disclosure of God that generates faith and shapes the consciousness of the community. Analogical developmentalism takes revelation to disclose information about the interaction and dynamic operations of God, the world, and humanity. Though biblical warrants exist for all these understandings of revelation, no single one is mandated by the Scriptures themselves.

About the concept of revelation each view of biblical authority must be explicit and clear. In the next two chapters I will clarify the understanding of revelation, religious knowledge, and inspiration that function as ingredients in the theory of biblical authority I espouse.

Part Two

Toward a
Contemporary View

4

The Bible in
Postmodern Culture

Previous chapters have sketched some modern values and have indicated how they challenge the post-Reformation understanding of the authority of the Bible. Their challenge has called forth several responses, each of which forms the nucleus of a theory of biblical authority. Six such theories have been outlined, four viable for the church and two not.

Any theory of biblical authority coordinates two sets of appeals: one to selected features of the Bible and the other to selected characteristics of the society contemporary with the theory. Each position discussed in chapters 2 and 3—supernaturalism, evangelicalism, ecclesial developmentalism, and analogical developmentalism—appeals to something that is more credible than tradition in the eyes of those imbued with modern culture: personal experience, the history of the community, observable events from the past, or the way things work in the world. The objective in every case is to secure a solid footing on which to build a theory of authority, a footing that seems to be more scientific than beliefs or dogmas are.

All theories of biblical authority involve extrabiblical appeals to values or assumptions held by the prevailing culture. As the values and assumptions change from one cultural epoch to another, new or revised understandings of biblical authority are needed. It is necessary to take the cultural context seriously in developing, adopting, and using any theory of biblical authority. Postmodern culture is gradually superseding modern culture. The appeals made by the four positions workable in the modern church do not have the weight for postmodern culture that they did for modern. A contemporary theory of biblical authority must seek a new grounding in order to do in postmodern society what the four theories were able to do in modern. A new understanding of biblical authority is necessary, one better attuned to the postmodern outlook.

The present chapter discusses our current cultural context and endeavors to isolate features that will influence my theory of biblical authority. Two cautions are in order. First, when a theory of biblical authority takes account of contemporary cultural developments, it does not necessarily endorse those developments or find them beneficial. To underline that point, this chapter focuses on certain problematic characteristics of our present society to which features of the Bible can be correlated. Second, my account of the present is highly selective. Other observers may object, and may want to describe today's culture quite differently. Disagreements of this kind are important, because they affect the content and emphasis of any theory of biblical authority, but they do not negate the basic procedural point, that theories of biblical authority inevitably employ selected features of their contemporary culture and that those features should be specified and assessed.

The Postmodern Age

Increasingly we are living in a postmodern age. Since World War I in Europe and somewhat later in the United States, a shift has been occurring in Western culture. The confidence and optimism of the modern age have largely disappeared. There are a number of reasons for this:

■ Devastating wars have been fought. As Richard Rubenstein observes, tactics aimed at the mass annihilation of enemy forces have in the twentieth century replaced the sophisticated strategies by which previous wars were fought and won.[1] "Never before," he laments, "have human beings been so expendable."[2]

■ Nuclear power, with its awesome destructiveness, is a besetting presence. Since 1945 the world has lived with the menace of a nuclear catastrophe of apocalyptic proportions.

■ There has been a growing awareness of cultural diversity. Partly owing to colonialism, a large store of information about non-European cultures has been amassed in the past 175 years. At first it seemed possible to regard these cultures as inferior, but gradually their independent value has had to be acknowledged. As a result, Western perspectives no longer seem objective and universal.

■ In science significant changes have occurred that have influenced people's perceptions of the world. Heisenberg's indeterminacy principle, Einstein's theory of relativity, and numerous other revolutionary developments have robbed the world of its Newtonian stability. Biological evolution and the Darwinian theory of the survival of the fittest have called into question the essential harmony of human and animal life on this planet. The moral law and the natural law as applied to human beings seem at odds with each other, and instability seems to rule.

■ The Holocaust has occurred, perpetrated by one of the most "civilized" of European nations. The news that some eleven million noncombatants were systematically put to death has shocked the world into a realization that something basic has gone wrong. It has become more difficult to believe that human beings are inherently good and require only education in order to make social progress. Though information concerning the Holocaust was available in the 1940s, not until about 1960 was the event widely studied. Only then did its far-reaching implications begin to be felt by large numbers of Americans.

■ The twentieth century has been marked by the growing influence of Freud and Marx, whose ideologies challenge the supremacy of reason at the same time that they reflect it. In the light of the theories of Freud and Marx, human beings seem less the masters of their fate than they seemed earlier, and more influenced by subconscious and economic forces.

■ The pervasive influence of movies and television has reduced the sense of temporal sequence. The novel was a literary medium typical of the modern age. In novels that employ a classical structure, events are presented sequentially. (More recently some novels—perhaps influenced by postmodern awareness—have abandoned their classical, time-oriented structure.) Historical accounts follow the same pattern. By their very nature, however, films, television, and videotapes present the world differently. One image can follow another without regard to temporal sequence. A film can mix contemporary events with documentary footage several decades old. "Sesame Street" jumps from one ninety-second spot to another without chronological sequence or any other apparent order. A television program about the Roman Empire is interrupted with commercials about the latest improvement in automobiles and a news report about astronauts. The reduced sense of temporal sequence in films and television is important, because the images on the screen are often more real to people than the lives they live; they act out the images they see. The more television people watch, for example, the more distorted and exaggerated is their perception of the prevalence of crime where they live. What is presented on television and how it is presented have deeply influenced twentieth-century perceptions of the world.

■ New industrial patterns have fractured old communities and created a new degree of individualism. Persons are no longer tied into an overarching framework of meaning about which there is community consensus. They have been isolated and left to develop an individualized philosophy and set of values. Or they have been linked into "electronic gatherings," where they share an experience but have no personal contact—in other words, where no genuine community develops.

Overall, the impression is that "things fall apart; the centre cannot hold,"[3] or to change the metaphor, that things are coming apart at the seams. And this has influenced perceptions of what is and can be authoritative.

The Foundations of a Postmodern Theory

The four workable theories about biblical authority that were developed during the modern age buttressed the authority of the Bible by bracing it to one or another principle about which the modern age felt confident. As postmodernism replaces modern culture, however, confidence in those principles slips, eroding the persuasiveness of the four theories.

We are left in a quandary. On the one hand, a new theory is called for. On the other hand, postmodern culture presents us with no certainties to which biblical authority can be lashed. The character of the entire task is thus different from what it was for those addressing modern culture, and perhaps somewhat more difficult. It is necessary to begin anew, laying the foundations of a new theory amid the sands of uncertainty; one cannot merely refurbish an old theoretical edifice.

Chapter 6 will argue that authority is a byproduct of a relationship that develops over time in which a community learns to trust someone or something it finds useful and appropriate to its tasks. In a postmodern age authority is generated anew as the Bible is used and its usefulness is rediscovered. No contemporary theory of the authority of the Bible can assume that a person will be convinced of the Bible's authority apart from participation in the community of faith. As Jaroslav Pelikan observed after hearing his eight-year-old daughter sing, "Jesus loves me, this I know, for the Bible tells me so," the lyrics of the children's song were incorrect for her. She had not read the Bible. She knew that Jesus loved her because her mother, her father, her Sunday-school teacher, her pastor, and others in the Christian community had told her so. Only later would she some into contact with the Bible.[4]

Here another quandary meets us. On the one hand, authority relationships develop only within a community. On the other hand, postmodern society lacks strong communities and provides its members with very little experience of what living in community is like, thus making if difficult for many outside the church, and some within it, to understand the dynamics of genuine authority. Much of the energy of the modern age went into freeing individuals from the constraints of arbitrary traditions. In this the modern age succeeded so well that individuals have been left without strong community ties.[5] The result has been the isolation of seemingly autonomous individuals.

The church introduces people to the experience of living in community with others. A postmodern theory of biblical authority needs to begin with the lived reality of a community of faith. What the church must offer this age is a humane community in which diversity is respected. As Paul eloquently argues in 1 Corinthians, and Matthew advocates in his own way in his Gospel, the church ought to be a community in which an undergirding unity ties together quite different kinds of people. Christian community involves unity without uniformity. By modeling humane community, the church can supply something very important to a postmodern age—not, to be sure, something consciously sought but something missing and genuinely needed by isolated postmodern individuals.

Few in the contemporary world go looking for close community ties, since most are not even aware of the absence of such ties until they have been experienced.[6] Our society elevates all sorts of individualistic images—the Lone Ranger, the Marlboro Man, the Bionic Woman, Superman—but very few of authentic community. We receive virtually no signals from popular culture that strong community ties create strong individuals and that we all need community. Not since the communes of the counter culture in the early 1970s has community-formation received much attention in our society.

As a humane community, the church is the context within which the Scriptures can assume authority, authority at least of the kind appropriate to the Bible's character and the tasks of the church. The authors of *Habits of the Heart* confirm the important contribution the church can make to our society:

> The great contribution that the church idea can make today is its emphasis on the fact that individuality and society are not opposites but require each other. It was perhaps necessary at a certain stage in the development of modern society for individuals to declare their independence from churches, states, and families. But absolute independence becomes the atomism Tocqueville feared, a condition for a new despotism worse than the old. The church idea reminds us that in our independence we count on others and helps us see that a healthy, grown-up independence is one that admits to healthy grown-up dependence on others. Absolute independence is a false ideal. It delivers not the autonomy it promises but loneliness and vulnerability instead. Concomi-

> tantly, the church idea reminds us that authority
> need not be external and oppressive. It is something
> we can participate in. . . . A church that can be
> counted on and can count on its members can be a
> great source of strength in reconstituting the social
> basis of our society.[7]

The authors go on to say that the church idea needs to be modified by insights from sectarian religion, where the goals of purity and social reform have been preserved. They believe that a healthy Christian community will nourish and sustain a healthy religious individualism, which will equip people to deal with society and give them the inner spiritual strength and discipline not available from secular individualism.

The nurture of community is therefore both a way of fostering a setting within which authority can develop and a genuine contribution to postmodern society. In the context of community a theory can be developed that links features of the Bible with features of contemporary life.

The Scriptures can function as an authority in the life of the church without a consciously thought-out theory of their authority, but a consciously thought-out theory is important in the long run. For it keeps the church from obscuring or misinterpreting the contribution the Bible can make to its life and tasks. A good theory makes room for the Bible to do its work. This chapter will endeavor to sketch a specifically postmodern theory of the Bible's authority.

As we have already seen, any theory of scriptural authority involves appeals to extrabiblical notions regarded as credible by contemporary consciousness. Any theory therefore brings together selected features of contemporary consciousness and selected features of the Bible and its message. A theory is persuasive to the degree that it (a) perceives with insight and sensitivity the character of contemporary consciousness, (b) perceives with insight and clarity one or more features of the Bible, and (c) brings the character of contemporary consciousness and the features of the Bible into a telling conjunction such that the helpfulness of the Bible will be evident.

As a preliminary to an adequate theory, I will here identify three characteristics of contemporary postmodern consciousness, to each of which I will relate a significant feature of the Bible and its message.

The Lack of Transcendence

One characteristic of postmodern consciousness is its lack of any sense of transcendence. The modern age unleashed a heady sense of human freedom and power. People felt emancipated from age-old political, economic, and social traditions. It was the age of revolution, the time for human beings to take charge and create more "rational" patterns. An unintended consequence, however, was the loss of any sense of transcendence. Sometimes that meant atheism, but more often there was no denial of God's existence. Instead, God was subordinated or marginalized. Loyalty to God no longer stood above loyalty to the state or to an ideology or a party. God was either compartmentalized— removed from contact with societal and political loyalties—or invoked only to serve and support them.

The lack of a sense of transcendence, then, is the absence of any effective loyalty to something or someone beyond oneself, beyond one's nation, party, vocation, or ideology. It leaves society with no limits to the exercise of human freedom and the aggrandizement of human power. "Secular gospels" and totalitarianisms are the result. The task in the postmodern age is not to turn back the clock or impose limits on freedom but to find some authentic sense of transcendence that will guide the exercise of human freedom and prevent its destructive excesses.

Not only is the postmodern age aware that it has no sense of transcendence but God's absence is now often experienced as tragic and painful rather than liberating and exhilarating. Contemporary human beings have witnessed the consequences of emancipation from transcendence. They have seen it in the totalitarian pretensions of countless governments and in the extermination of eleven million noncombatants during the Nazi Holocaust. They have seen it in the nightmare of threatened nuclear annihilation and in the seemingly inexorable illogic of the arms race. As John Pawlikowski puts it,

> At least indirectly, Western liberal thought was responsible for the Holocaust. By breaking the tight hold the God-concept had on previous generations, it paved the way for greater human freedom and self-sufficiency without realistically assessing the potential of the destructive forces within mankind to pervert this freedom into the cruelty revealed by the Nazi experiment. Thus, the Holocaust shattered much of the grandeur of Western liberal thought. In some ways it represents the ultimate achievement of the person totally "liberated" from God.[8]

The task is "to find a way to affirm the new sense of human freedom that is continuing to dawn while channeling it into constructive outlets."[9]

The loss of a sense of transcendence has had its effect on Christian theology. From classical and medieval thought, premodern Christian theology had acquired a particular concept of God—the concept of "classical theism," characterized by notions of God's aseity, unchangeableness, omniscience, omnipotence, infinity, and passionlessness. That concept went largely unchallenged in the Reformation period (though it did seem to impede Luther in *The Bondage of the Will*),[10] the post-Reformation era, and the modern age. Not until the second half of the nineteenth century did it come into question, and not until the twentieth century were philosophical and theological alternatives to it developed. Today classical theism is no longer self-evident. To fill the void of the postmodern era and renew a sense of transcendence, a concept of God must be chastened by the criticisms of the modern age and the tragedies of the twentieth century.

Where can we find the materials for the reconstruction that is needed? A postmodern theory of biblical authority suggests that we turn to the Bible. What is there, of course, is not a ready-made doctrine of God. Instead there are documents transparent to the identity and character of God, an identity and character communicated as much by metaphor as by precise specification.[11] Classical theism selected certain metaphors from the Scriptures and discredited others as anthropomorphism. It considered God to be unchanging, but only by closing its eyes to the thirty-odd references in the Hebrew Scriptures divine repenting, that is, to changes in God's mind or plans. Not only is classical theism inadequate to the needs of the postmodern age, it does not represent the full biblical witness. The Bible provides a full range of metaphors with which to reconstruct the concept of God.

The Scriptures are, as I shall argue, a set of documents whose words have been stretched and pulled, edited and refined, to the point where they are transparent to the presence and identity of God. They are therefore admirably well suited to addressing postmodern human beings who are out of touch with transcendence.

For the Scriptures to be useful in reacquainting human beings with transcendence, it is not necessary to demonstrate the Bible's internal consistency or the accuracy of its historical reports; an inner miracle need not be experienced; no demonstration of the place of biblical documents in the history of the community is necessary; nor must there be an antecedent conviction that they correlate with a philosophical portrait of the world in process. What was invoked in support of the theories constructed during the modern age does not contribute to the renewed sense of transcendence that is desperately needed in the postmodern age.

No Overarching Story

A second characteristic of postmodern consciousness is the absence of any overarching "story"—that is, of any sense of the direction in which society as a whole ought to be heading and of one's own role in its movement. Joan Didion, a journalist and author from California, tells of being on a flight from Los Angeles to Hawaii in 1975. While the plane was still on the ground preparing for its departure, a man behind her screamed at a woman who seemed to be his wife and then left the plane. Airline employees rushed on and off, and there was considerable confusion. Didion reports that she kept thinking about the incident as the plane crossed the Pacific:

> It was not until we had passed Diamond Head and were coming over the reef for landing at Honolulu, however, that I realized what I most disliked about this incident: I disliked it because it had the aspect of a short story, one of those "little epiphany" stories in which the main character glimpses a crisis in a stranger's life—a woman weeping in a tearoom, often, or an accident seen from the window of a train, "tearooms" and "trains" still being fixtures of short stories although not of real life—and is moved to see his or her own life in a new light. I was not going to Honolulu because I wanted to see life reduced to a short story. I was going to Honolulu because I wanted to see life expanded to a novel, and I still do.[12]

In the context of *The White Album* as a whole, Didion's remarks illustrate her sense that she does not have an overarching story with which to make sense of her life or the incidents she observes and reports. She wants and needs to see her "life expanded to a novel." A short story is inadequate; it can unpack a moment but not the whole. Because a "little epiphany" recounts a shift in perspective, even it presupposes an overarching story. Without that frame of reference, what may serve as a "little epiphany" for an imaginary character cannot be so for her. The incident remains an unconnected fragment, another in a sequence of episodes that do not come together into a coherent, meaningful novel or a life-encompassing story.

Didion is, in my judgment, typical of postmoderns. Without an overarching story, contemporary human beings cope by adopting a privatized individualism in which "one's own idiosyncratic preferences are their own justification, because they define the true self."[13] Here

79

"utility replaces duty; self-expression unseats authority. 'Being good' becomes 'feeling good.'"[14]

Now, a prominent feature of the Scriptures is that they tell the story of God and God's people. The Bible not only characterizes God's identity but also gives some indication of God's past involvement with people and some vision of what the future ought to be like. From the priestly author's perception that God is moving the world toward Sabbath rest, to the prophet's promise of a shalom in which the lion lies down with the lamb and swords are beaten into plowshares and spears into pruning hooks, to the apocalyptic vision of the arrival on earth of the heavenly city devoid of tears and fear and totally transparent to God's presence, the Scriptures portray not only the past but also the future goal of God's relationship with God's people. The biblical authors stretch their perception of God back to essay human beginnings and forward to imagine human endings, all to give some sense of the grand novel—to use Didion's word—or epic story within which each believer discovers an identity and is given an important role.

The Scriptures function in the community of faith not primarily as historical documents but mainly as identity-forming stories. The stories issue from the community's struggle with a series of identity-forming revelatory events and are transparent enough to those events to make a claim on their readers and hearers. The stories give perspective to the community into which the individual is more and more deeply drawn. As part of that community, a person senses the source and the goal of life, a source that is both past and present and a goal that is both present and future.

The modern theories examined in chapters 2 and 3 all appeal to personal or collective history. History may be used to ground a tradition, but if it is the sort of history arising from careful academic study it cannot satisfy the need for an overarching story.[15] An identity-forming story ultimately involves a larger perspective, one including God and the whole universe—that is, one including, alongside the historic, the prehistoric, the suprahistoric, and the posthistoric. The story is told with an eye toward the meaning of the hearer's existence rather than toward academic precision. The appeal to history still has a place in our postmodern approach to the Bible, but it cannot by itself meet the postmodern need for an overarching story.

Instead of finding comfort by historicizing Genesis into the "science" of creationism or by historicizing Revelation into a timetable for the future, the postmodern age finds meaning in a vision of the past and future that can ground humane values without destroying human freedom, dignity, or creativity. The community experience and the overarching story provided by the Scriptures join to inform Christian identity and to overcome the disorientation accompanying the experiences of the twentieth century. An overarching story may not provide security from problems and tragedies, but it does provide an orientation, it does locate the individual and give meaning to the whole.

The Disappearance of Humane Values

A third characteristic of postmodern consciousness is its growing cognition of the disappearance of societal consensus about and support for certain humane values. The modern age assumed that people of reason would choose what was right. Standards of right and wrong seemed universally evident and valid. An enlightened populace would automatically produce a humane society. In the postmodern age confidence on that point has disappeared.

Look again at Nazi Germany. Several commanders of the *Einsatzgruppen*, who followed the German armies into eastern Europe to round up Jews and Gypsies, shoot them, and bury their bodies in mass graves, were well educated. "Of the first four Einsatzgruppen commanders, three had Ph.D. degrees. . . . A number of lesser officers were also university educated. One was a pastor."[16] Medical doctors performed painful and sometimes lethal experiments on prison-camp inmates and reported their findings to learned societies without eliciting any protests from their educated colleagues.[17] People of reason seemed unable to discern what was right for a humane society and for their role in it.

Even in medieval pogroms a moral barrier existed to protect human life, and lives were lost only when order broke down. Government authorities intervened to end the killing and punish wrongdoers. In the twentieth century the barrier against killing has been breached. In the Holocaust it became possible to organize a government project the only purpose of which was to exterminate human life. Indeed, trains essential to the war effort were diverted to the mass-killing operations. As Richard Rubenstein argues, this was not an aberration but a culmination of many tendencies inherent in Western society. Because the Nazis ruptured the barrier, mass extermination has become a possibility that other governments will consider. Rubenstein warns,

> Until ethical theorists and theologians are prepared
> to face without sentimentality the kind of action it is
> possible freely to perpetrate under conditions of
> utter respectability in an advanced, contemporary

society, none of their assertions about the existence
of moral norms will have much credibility. To
repeat, no laws were broken and no crimes were
committed at Auschwitz. Those who were
condemned to the society of total domination were
stripped of all protection of the law before they
entered. Finally, no credible punishment was meted
out. Truly, the twentieth century has been the
century par excellence that is *beyond good and evil*.[18]

I once asked a class of mine, which had spent half a semester
studying life in the camps, to role-play the board of directors of a large
corporation. They were to decide whether to build a factory in a prison
camp. The rewards for saying yes would be cheaper labor and greater
profits than competing firms enjoyed. The only consequence of saying
no would be the obligation to explain their decision to the company's
stockholders, with the risk of losing their places on the board. They discussed the decision and, much to my distress, voted to build the factory.
In the discussion that followed, they explained that I had asked them to
play a role and that when they thought about it realistically they did not
have the courage to jeopardize their positions on the board. They therefore voted yes even though the vote would cause misery for others. Their
honesty was gratifying, but their priorities were all too reminiscent of
recent reality.

The loss of humane values means the readiness to inflict significant harm on others when it is politically, economically, or vocationally
expedient to do so. Relativism seems to reign. Cultural and societal
diversity have influenced postmoderns so profoundly that they think
they must tolerate virtually any behavior by others and dare not pre-
sume to assess the adequacy of anyone else's moral decisions. College
students confronting the Holocaust, for example, experience a disturb-
ing choice. Their socialization tells them not to judge the behavior of
others, particularly others living under circumstances very different from
their own. Yet their every instinct makes them feel what the Nazis did
to their victims was wrong and that it was wrong for a young camp inmate
to steal bread from his father.

Awash in a sea of relativism, anchored only by utilitarian individualism, postmoderns lack the resources to address the crucial issues
of our day,[19] most of which require the help of clear societal norms and
standards. As Geoffrey Vickers has observed,

> To control the flooding of the Thames we had only to
> discipline the river. To control its pollution we have
> to discipline ourselves and notably the industrial

processes which are the pride of our technology. This poses not technological but political and cultural problems.[20]

Societal norms are needed as a basis for the political process.

The Bible does not prescribe solutions for the perplexing issues of our day or supply ready-made answers to every difficulty, but it does offer the framework within which to address them. The Bible is paradigmatic in that it portrays men and women struggling to ascertain the societal implications of the identity of God and of the overarching story of God's relations with humankind. The Bible shows how certain human beings derived from the identity of God the standards that would govern their own behavior as a community of faith and the standards by which they would assess the behavior of peoples beyond the boundaries of their own community.

For the most part, the Scriptures are clear that the two sets of standards are not identical. The community itself is called to holiness, that is, to a level of servanthood not expected of human beings unaware of God's acts in their behalf. Those outside the community of faith are expected to subscribe to norms of justice and respect for human dignity that are lodged in the fabric of what it means to be human. Thus the political and cultural task for the people of God is not to Christianize but to humanize (that is, to see that justice is done and human dignity is enhanced in) the larger society of which they are a part.

The community of faith is the laboratory in which appropriate priorities are constructed and refined. A set of humane values is there developed to offer the larger postmodern society, not by imposing them or even assuming that they are universally valid but by modeling them and offering them freely. The church becomes one of several religious or ethically humanistic groups offering the larger society concrete embodiments of humane values, out of which a new ethical consensus may be fashioned. (Recall how during the energy crisis of the 1970s the simple living of the Mennonites became a model for others to follow.)

It is not easy to specify all that the constructing and refining of priorities implies. But the point is that the Bible, properly understood and properly interpreted, provides resources upon which to proceed with that task.

The Whole Bible

Three characteristics of postmodern society have been identified: the loss of a sense of transcendence, the need for an overarching story, and the disappearance of an undergirding consensus regarding humane values in society. A theory that seeks to relate the Bible to this context must affirm clearly the importance of the old Testament as well as the New. The New Testament assumes an acquaintance with so much that pertains to these topics that by itself it is an inadequate resource for responding to the needs of a postmodern age.

Although some of what I say in the following chapters has reference more directly to the New Testament than to the old, I intend my theory as a whole to affirm as clearly as possible the canonical status of both testaments. However illumining Jesus the Christ may be for understanding the character and identity of God, I do not take the importance of the Old Testament to derive solely from the Christ-event or depend upon verification of the Old Testament's contents in the New. The good news is found throughout the Bible, not just in the New Testament.

In this regard even the nomenclature is a stumbling block. The title Old Testament seems to carry the connotation of something out-of-date, but this impression is misleading. Its contents are very relevant to contemporary society and should not be overlooked by the church. Nor should the Old Testament be interpreted only by those within the church. The insights of Jewish scholars are also very important, not only to help illumine the text but also to help refurbish the church's sense of its Jewish roots and thereby undergird the integrity of its prophetic witness in any cultural setting, our own included.

A complete discussion of the relationship between the Old and the New Testaments is not necessary for our task. What does need to be affirmed is that both testaments are important in addressing the needs of postmodern society. Both contribute to our understanding of the identity of God, the community of faith, and the priorities appropriate for human society, and no overarching story can be constructed without insights drawn from the whole of Scripture, from Genesis to Revelation.

Modern Theories in a Postmodern Setting

How do modern theories of biblical authority function in a postmodern society? For present purposes, we can simplify—so long as we recognize that this is what we are doing—the four options into two: a "conservative" view, which combines elements of supernaturalism and evangelicalism, and a "critical" view, which combines the two developmentalist models.

In a postmodern society, the conservative alternative perceives at least part of the problem. It recognizes the relativism, the secularism, the disorientation, and certain facets of the individualism of postmodern human beings. But it recoils from the features it recognizes rather than empathizing with or letting itself "be with" those caught up in them. The solution recommended by the conservative position involves assent to an authoritarian view of the Bible, one that imposes upon the church and, often, upon society one particular historical embodiment of the kingdom of God. It selects from the cluster of confessional embodiments found in the Bible a unitary set of standards (e.g., in favor of capital punishment or patriarchal families), absolutizes its selection, and imposes the standards on contemporary human beings. Its unitary set of standards may include both teachings (e.g., a particular theory of the atonement) and ethical standards.

The authoritarian character of this approach is attractive to some postmoderns who feel their age's disorientation especially deeply. They can sometimes be convinced that adherence to absolute standards is the only alternative to relativism. One difficulty, though, is that political force is necessary for imposing absolute standards on a postmodern society. That spells tyranny and does not address the problems generated by the three characteristics of postmodern consciousness I have described: the loss of a sense of transcendence, the lack of an overarching story, and the disappearance of humane values.

Another difficulty is that the impact created by the authoritarian approach is inconsistent with the impact created by the words recorded within the Bible itself. In *The Diversity of Scripture*, Paul Hanson discusses two different tendencies in the Bible: one more dynamic (oriented toward "reform") and the other more static (oriented toward "form"). Though both tendencies have to be acknowledged in any encompassing view of the Scriptures and the church, the static is penultimate; by itself it is unable to represent the message of the Scriptures:

> To argue for the immutability of existing forms is to subscribe to the "golden age" mentality of myth which Hebrew religion supplanted; it is to betray the rich diversity of our heritage; and above all it is to deny the dynamic movement which our ancestors discerned running through all space and time. To freeze symbolism is to announce that the Kingdom of God has fully arrived, that no groups remain excluded by our present structures, that we need anticipate no further prophets and teachers to challenge and reform. Such a position is uneschatological, unbiblical.[21]

The authoritarian impact of a conservative view of the Bible aggressively applied in a postmodern age is inconsistent with the consequences of the message of God evidenced within the Scriptures themselves.

In a postmodern society the critical theory of biblical authority has a different difficulty. It tends to emphasize the pastness of the writings, the historical and cultural distance between the world of the biblical documents and our own. It tends also to play down the symbolic aspects of the biblical story, seeking the solid stuff provided by a clear, well-informed, historical reading of the documents. Nothing is wrong with that. But it provides no direct way to address the postmodern age. An imaginative, creative use of the biblical symbols and metaphors is needed to begin constructing a revised doctrine of God, to articulate the overarching story, and to fortify the humane values that must be urged on the postmodern age. The imagination must always be disciplined by critical-historical investigation, but a critical outlook alone is ill suited to undertaking imaginative reconstruction.

Furthermore, the critical approach shelters many of the values that are now up for reconsideration and reevaluation—though not abandonment—in the postmodern age. It is aligned with the modern protest against authority. It is intent on protecting the rights of the individual over against the group. It esteems technical competence. The critical mind-set is ill prepared to diagnose and address postmodern problems, because to do so it must call into question the adequacy of some of the very values it most cherishes.

Both the conservative and the critical approaches to the authority of the Bible leave the individual largely passive. Both seek to convince and reassure the individual, and both deem the passive acceptance of the authority of the Bible a sufficient foundation for Christian faith and theology.

Active Participation

A postmodern theory is more active in at least three ways:

1. Biblical authority in the postmodern age cannot be braced to some fixed principle, because postmodern culture offers none. Instead, a postmodern theory invites individuals to "try on" the Christian message by participating in the Christian community. It is not expected that they will accept the authority of the Bible first and then believe the Christian gospel. Rather, believers catch sight of the gospel and are transformed by its message before being confronted with the question of the authority of the Scriptures. The decision concerning biblical

authority is therefore made on the basis of the existential depth and adequacy of the Christian message over against other religious or quasi-religious options. At this level, no neutral bench marks are available, there is only open-eyed involvement. In every century since Christendom—defined as a culture and a sociopolitical order based explicitly on Christian principles and values—was established, the church and the Scriptures have needed only to influence and reform the identities of persons already shaped by a congenial culture. Christendom has ended, however, and its demise makes the task somewhat more difficult. Identities now need to be formed amid a prevailing disorientation, a deep existential confusion, and a lack of overarching direction. The identity formation cannot be achieved passively; active involvement is crucial, for an identity is created only within a relationship and only as that relationship grows and matures. To become a Christian in the contemporary age is more a matter of praxis than the result of intellectual argument based on commonly accepted norms.

2. In the absence of any consensus regarding the concept of God, the believer is invited to participate in the construction or reconstruction of a doctrine that is more viable for postmodern, post-Holocaust times than classical theism is and more inclusive of the full range of biblical metaphors and images. The believer is not asked to accept a ready-made package but is called to participate actively and thoughtfully in the study and appropriation of Scripture and the insightful analysis of contemporary society.

3. So long as classical theism reigned, the believer could be asked to acquiesce to the rule and dominion of God. God was above it all and firmly in control. The believer's role was passive acceptance. If, however, as I shall argue in chapter 5, the emphasis needs to be placed not on the power but on the presence of God, a postmodern understanding will likely perceive God to be an active but noncontrolling participant in history. In response to the emphasis on God's presence, the believer will be called to action, not only to articulate and communicate God's identity but also to contribute to the renewal of the world. Because God created human beings with freedom and called them to participate actively in the overarching goal of the kingdom, God's power is to some extent dependent upon the divine ability to persuade human beings

to become partners in restoring shalom to the world. God thus is understood to inspire and undergird human efforts to create a more humane world. Moreover, God is seen to coexperience every joy and tragedy that occurs in those efforts. God can suffer defeat, as during the Holocaust, but even in the midst of defeat God is present with us human beings. Though the ultimate authority in the life of the believer, God does not exercise an authoritarian influence. A postclassical doctrine of God emphasizes the divine presence and the interdependence of God and human beings. It calls for more active human involvement than does classical theory.

Likewise a postmodern approach to the authority of the Bible presupposes the active participation of each believer. To the degree that each believer is active in the tasks appropriate to God's kingdom, an authority relationship develops between the Bible and the believer, which is neither created by individual decision nor imposed from without. The usefulness of the Bible becomes evident as the believer engages in the appropriate tasks.

A Postmodern Theory

If a theory of the authority of the Bible brings selected features of contemporary society into correlation with selected features of the Bible, then we have here the makings of a contemporary theory. The new theory does not look exactly like the modern theories, but its formal components are similar.

Postmodern society is characterized by a loss of the sense of transcendence, by the absence of any overarching story, and by the disappearance of the undergirding structure that supports humane values and knits together individuals. In sum, it is marked by individualism. The theory I have sketched here correlates these features with the Scriptures' transparency to the presence and identity of God, with the story or narrative character of the Bible (as distinguished from its historicity), and with the contributions the Bible makes to a humane, nonauthoritarian set of values exhibiting a scope and basis more encompassing than just individual preference. This theory calls for active involvement by the individual in the community, the construction or reconstruction of a doctrine of God, and the development of values congruent with the new doctrine. An authority relationship is a byproduct of participation in the community and in its tasks.

5

God's Presence, Revelation, and Inspiration

Why We Need a Contemporary View of the Bible

Every theory of biblical authority involves appeals to selected features of a culture, whether today's culture or that of some previous era. But such appeals, though inescapable, can be effective only when they engage values and assumptions that are currently persuasive. Cultural change is therefore one reason for formulating a new theory of biblical authority, a theory that takes into account postmodern assumptions.

A second reason is pastoral. Every theory of biblical authority affects the way the Bible is taught and understood in the church. An out-of-date view places an extra impediment in the way of the Scripture's message. A contemporary view cannot take the place of the Scriptures and do what only then can do, but it can clear the way for the Bible to perform its task more effectively. A proper contemporary view opens the way for persons to be confronted by the presence of God as it is mediated through the Scriptures rather than by issues or arguments or disputes rehearsed from a previous era which are by now of peripheral importance.

Another aspect of the pastoral need for an adequate conception of scriptural authority lies in the fact that differing theories of biblical authority result in differing conclusions regarding the ethical implications of the biblical texts for sexual behavior, gender roles, homosexuality, nuclear war, the proper role of government, and the like. A contemporary view is necessary in order that we may wend our way as carefully and judiciously as possible through the delicate considerations involved in specifying the insights of the Bible regarding these topics.

A third reason we need a contemporary view is that the Scriptures make several different kinds of claims. David Bartlett, for example, locates four major sorts of claim made by various parts of Scripture. They are claims made by (a) the authority of words ("Thus says the Lord"),

(b) the authority of deeds, (c) the authority of witness (e.g., Paul's reports of his call to apostleship), and (d) the authority of wisdom.[1] The variety in the kinds of claims can be handled in different ways. It is possible to restrict attention to those kinds which are most relevant to the present, to emphasize one or two and subordinate the others, or to try to integrate all into some overarching whole. In any case, a contemporary theory of biblical authority is needed in order to explain why one way is chosen rather than another.

Since any view of the authority of the Bible involves prior decisions about a number of related topics, this chapter will discuss the image of God's relation to the world, the character of revelation, the relationship of revelation to the spoken and written word, and the role of inspiration. The conclusions I reach here will set the stage for the contemporary theory of biblical authority that I am recommending.

David Kelsey claims to make no theological assertions when he analyzes the "uses of Scripture in recent theology."[2] His work is descriptive and analytic to the degree that he does not see himself endorsing a specific theological position. Unlike Kelsey, I will make recommendations that are overtly theological. The assertions I make and the positions I take in this chapter may not fit with every theology and every view of biblical authority. They are not neutral, but they are open to examination and challenge. The ultimate goal toward which the chapter moves is to outline a theological position regarding God's relation to the world, revelation, the articulation of revelation, and inspiration, and in so doing to illustrate the steps involved in creating a contemporary theory of biblical authority.

The Image of God's Relation to the World

Because any image of God's relation to the world is logically extrabiblical, it forms but one way of understanding the Bible. That is true not only of the images we have discussed previously but also of the model that I will present in this chapter. I make no claim that what I offer is the only correct view or the only view that will work in the present. Instead, it is *one* view that is both appropriate to Christian identity and formulated with the needs of the current generation in mind. It fits our context well enough not to place needless stumbling blocks in the path to the gospel. I acknowledge that my claims remain open to debate and that insights can be gleaned from observers who read our times differently.

To suggest that an image of God's relation to the world must be framed with contemporary society in mind does not mean that it must be derived from secular society. Secular society offers no workable images of God's relation to the world. Instead, any plausible image is generated by the intersection of Christian identity with contemporary culture. The two rub together in such a way as to make some images more plausible than others. Any model of God's relation to the world has a curious status: it is conditioned by Christian identity, which is influenced in dialogical ways by the Bible, at the same time that it is logically extra-biblical, influencing the way the Bible is understood. This is not entirely circular, because we do not encounter the Bible in isolation. Our sense of Christian identity is drawn from the faith community, with which we are in contact. Prior to our reading of the Scriptures, the images of God current in that community have influenced us. Although the images may have been suggested by passages in the Bible, they seldom embody the full range and depth of the biblical portrait of God and its implica-tions. The images thus still need to be revised and deepened by the scriptural witness at the same time that they influence the way we read the Scriptures.

An analogy may pull these comments together: I have an image of my father's relation to his children. It is, I have discovered, not exactly the same as the one carried by my brother or my sister. (The same is true of our images of our mother, of course.) My image, for example, is shaped by the fact that my father and I worked together day in and day out for at least three months a year until I was twenty-four years old. My sister's is shaped by the fact that she was with him mostly at meals or after work or on Sundays and holidays. My brother also worked with him, but their relationship was quite different, it seems, both because my brother was eleven years younger than I (and my father eleven years older when my brother reached any given age) and because my brother and I had different interests. My father apparently made significant adaptations to the individuality of his sons. We have different images in part because as he grew older his industriousness and impatience diminished, in part because my brother and I are different, in part because our father showed a slightly different face to each of us.

When my brother, sister, and I compare the images we have of our father, we discover in the surprising diversity a certain unity and plausibility. The images all seem to fit his identity in ways that patent distortions would not. We would, for example, reject in one voice a sug-gestion that he was unusually handsome or dishonest or petty. His identity was complex enough to allow for a considerable though not an unlimited variety of images. What holds them together is not their internal consistency but the whole to which each in its partial way points. It would be foolish for any one of us, having talked with the other children in the family, to claim that his or her own image was the only correct one. We agree on our father's warmth and his wisdom, his humor and integrity, but beyond that we make no effort to eliminate the diversity. Quite the contrary, our appreciation of our father's identity and character matures as our awareness of its complexity and adaptability increases.

I can push the analogy one step further. While our father was still alive, the image I had of him influenced how I interpreted and understood his words and actions. In some sense my image was logically prior to my understanding of any letter he wrote to me or any conversation we had. Yet it also grew out of my relationship with him; it changed and underwent adjustment as I related to him in new ways and understood him more deeply.

Only as we think about an image and test it do we come to recognize that it has been influencing perceptions even before we were aware of its presence. Its status is as curious as the before-and-after character of our image of God. We can neither escape its influence nor claim for it authoritative status. It is a product both of the other's identity and of our own spectacles that color what we see in that identity. The model I have of God's relation to the world, like the image I have of my father, is, in Kelsey's language, an "imaginative construal," workable but incomplete.

In the case of God, another complication enters: there are differing understandings of how we come to know God. On some understandings the Bible is believed to give us facts, either facts regarding the history of Israel and the early church from which an interpretation of God's acts in history can be inferred or facts regarding God's own deeds, God's supernatural interventions in history. On other understandings the Bible is seen to provide God-given propositional truths that can function as axioms for a theological system.

But another understanding of how humans come to know God is possible. Coming to know God is on this view a matter not of acquiring facts and working with them nor of affirming already formulated propositions but rather of articulating more clearly the identity of God. It is more like trying 'to put into words a portrait of one's spouse, more like trying to fathom the identity of another person, more a matter of "knowing who" than "knowing what" or "knowing how" or "knowing that." "Knowing who" gives us the kind of insight we get from great literature; it enhances our capacity to identify with another person and makes us different as a result. It may not equip us to do fractions any more quickly, it may not enable us to repair our car with ease, it may not add to our storehouse of information, but "knowing who" is still a kind of knowledge—indeed, in some ways, the most important kind.

What model of God's relation to the world will accompany the idea that coming to know God can be likened to other instances of "knowing who"? The focus here will be on God's presence. Presence is "being with" another or experiencing another's "being with" me. Presence may involve silence or speech. It may involve joint action, unilateral action, or even inaction. "Being with" has a variety of shapes and forms. In any of these, however, one person is touched by another. And the identity of the other is part and parcel of that presence. Revelation is the experience of God with us, of the presence of God.

Two stories may help add flavor to the way *presence* is used here. Mr. Smith (as we will call him) was in a hospital room, day after day, sitting with his wife who lay dying of cancer. The chaplain of the hospital stopped by once or twice each day. He fell into a pattern of sitting silently with Mr. Smith, saying nothing, only touching Mr. Smith's knee or shoulder as he arrived or left. Eventually Mrs. Smith died. After the funeral, Mr. Smith sought out the chaplain and in the most sincere and glowing terms imaginable thanked him "for all you did for me" during Mrs. Smith's hospitalization.[3] Hardly a word had been said: the chaplain's gift had been his presence.

When my own father died, a faculty colleague flew 350 miles to attend the funeral and to say a few words during the service. The family did not know he was coming until he was on his way. He could have sent a letter; instead he came in person to be with us in our grief. He spoke gracious, consoling words, but his most profound gift was his presence.

Similarly, the primary gift God gives human beings is God's presence. The presence cannot be seen objectively, though it is real and is filled with the identity of the one who is present. An objective observer in the wilderness may have seen only a cloud by day and a pillar of fire by night, but the people of Israel experienced God's presence in and with those signs. On the other hand, presence is not something exclusively subjective and inner. The one present confronts us, encounters us. The presence of another can change us and redirect our lives; it can alter our inner selves and is not a product merely of forces working within. Presence is neither external nor inward but a "coming together" with inner and outer ramifications.

The Character of Revelation

God is, at least potentially, present everywhere. The person who grows in grace experiences God's presence as ever more pervasive. Revelation, as I understand it, is a particular kind of presence: revelation is both an *identity-forming* presence, important because of its decisive initiating and shaping—or reshaping—impact, and a *community-forming* presence, whose impact is not merely private but corporate. Moses' encounter with the presence of God at the burning bush reshaped his own sense of purpose (cf. Exodus 3), propelling him back from Midian to his kinfolk in Egypt. But it also bequeathed to Israel the name and something of the identity of God. The experience was individual, its impact was corporate; Israel would henceforth be the people of Yahweh. Moses' encounter with the presence of God at Mount Sinai was even more clearly corporate in its significance: Israel would henceforth possess ten guidelines, ten clues to its identity as Yahweh's people. Revelation occurs when human beings experience in an identity-forming way the presence of God. What is shaped is not just the identity of an individual but the corporate identity of the people of God.

The presence of God affects one's sense of worth and one's sense of direction or purpose in life. The presence of God opens up persons, who can then *be with* other human beings in community. It provides, moreover, a focus around which members gather to explore, articulate, and embody their new identity. There they become who they are. Having been opened up to the presence of God, persons can also *be with* others outside their community, thereby mediating to outsiders the presence of God. In fact, this is the way most of us are first touched by the gospel—through the actions and words of someone whose identity has been shaped by revelation.

Revelation involves an *arresting* presence. God confronts us and pulls us up short; we must come to terms with this presence. We come to terms with God's presence through action and through words, through attempts to embody in actions and articulate in words what has been experienced. The endeavors often take time: appropriate words and actions may not present themselves immediately. We do not know how much searching was involved before Abraham set off for Canaan or Moses left Midian, but the story of Jeremiah shows a person hunting for words and actions to express and articulate God's presence amid the events of the day. No single thing Jeremiah did gave adequate expression to the presence he experienced. Carrying a yoke or burying underwear or visiting the king or debating the prophet's accusers—none of it came easily, though all flowed from Jeremiah's encounter with the arresting presence of God.

Revelation involves a *noncontrolling*, yet *powerful* presence. It does not dictate or determine but challenges, confronts, transforms, and enables. What comes through is the purposeful presence of God, which contains the priorities and goals that follow from a genuine concern for human wholeness and the welfare of all. Revelation is therefore an active presence, one that propels persons into empathic activity. The healed relationship instills a sense of the overall restoration of the world, and this sense reverberates its way through the identity of the faithful.

The presence of God is *relationship-forming*. Just as the presence of another person can touch us at a deep level and satisfy some unacknowledged longing, so the presence of God can engage us. It awakens in us an awareness of the emptiness we feel apart from God's presence. The power of the divine noncontrolling presence touches us so deeply that we feel somehow healed and drawn without coercion—yet also without conscious, premeditated choice—into relationship with God. The experience cannot be dismissed as a nice, one-time encounter. Humans in the presence of God feel that what is happening should go on. An internal struggle to make sense of a strange new longing ensues— a conflict between the will to autonomy and the profoundly satisfying experience of God's presence. The attracting power of the presence propels persons into a restored relationship with God.

The experience gives rise both to theories of predestination and to decision-oriented theologies. The presence of God is arresting. It attracts us without any prior choice on our part. Hence the images of predestination. If, however, the mental conflict results in the triumph of relationship over autonomy, of faith over denial, it seems more like a decision. Hence the appeal of decision-oriented theologies.

The Cultural Context

I do not put forward the understanding of revelation as presence arbitrarily but suggest that it is in harmony with the character of our times. Though contemporary culture does not dictate what image of God we should adopt, the cultural setting does appropriately affect decisions regarding which aspect of God's self-disclosure is to be taken as most central. For instance, the German Reformation in the early sixteenth century, in response to the basic problems of fear and guilt, focused its attention on God's attitude toward humans. Though fear and guilt are by no means nonexistent in our own day, they seem less central, especially for those outside the church. This is true in part because an awareness of sin depends upon a prior sense of God and God's righteousness. More central to today's society is the perception of God's absence.

We experience God's absence as our own disorientation. Things do not cohere for us, they lack direction and differentiated meaning. In the vacuum, we choose something of individual though not overarching value; we are "into" this or that and indifferent to other people's priorities as they "do their own thing." Each pursuit is, after all, no more than an individual preference.

Many cultural factors contribute to our disorientation and sense of God's absence. Among them is the legacy of a modern culture that viewed the world as one large, impersonal machine that left individuals to find their own way. Another reflects a postmodern rebellion against the modern claim of universal objectivity. If a standard is set too high, disillusionment occurs when it cannot be realized. The disillusionment accompanying the breakdown of modern culture has helped to produce a prevailing relativism.

In the United States another cultural factor contributing to our disorientation and sense of God's absence is the disintegration of the civil religion that provided a way for many to feel connected with the divine. It assumed as a matter of course that individual success was good for American society and that a strong America was good for God's purposes in the world. The 1960s and 1970s severed both links—the link tying the individual to the nation and the link tying the nation to God. Without those ties, many Americans are bewildered and no longer sense a meaningful connection of their lives with the divine.

In addition to our disorientation and the sense of God's absence, there is in our time an individual isolation. This feature of postmodern life has been an unforeseen byproduct of technology. As Daniel Boorstin points out, "progress" has taken us from stagecoaches, where half a dozen passengers spent hours together with nothing to do but talk with each other, to jumbo jets, where hundreds of passengers sit listening to individual headsets tuned to the music or movie of their choice.[4] Isolation rules. Anyone old enough to remember the introduction of television is aware that it has destroyed the patterns that existed of visiting one's neighbors during the winter months. On the frontier, people needed to get together for quilting bees, barn raisings, threshing bees, and the like. Affluence and technology have made independence possible, both in rural areas and in the suburbs. On a more substantive level, the breakdown of an accepted, shared set of priorities has left individuals feeling isolated and alone. The loneliness of our day is the loneliness of persons living shoulder to shoulder with an anonymous mass of humanity. It is the loneliness that comes from feeling faceless and unrecognized and from being buffeted by impersonal forces. The gift of presence is an antidote to isolation and loneliness. To understand God as presence is to employ a model that relates divine revelation in a direct and immediate way to the sense of absence underlying contemporary loneliness and disorientation.

There is also in contemporary culture a struggle to understand suffering, especially the massive suffering humankind has encountered in the twentieth century.[5] Suffering has shattered the optimism of modern culture and contributed to the emergence of the postmodern age. The understanding of God's revelation as presence responds no less to this feature of contemporary society. God can be seen to be with the sufferers coexperiencing their pain and agony. I know of no more powerful and existentially significant way to conceive God's relationship to the victims of the massive, destructive power plays of our time than to say that God is present with them, coexperiencing their torment. For those in pain, statements regarding the all-controlling power of God only make God seem the more absent. "If all-powerful, why does God not remove this suffering? What have I done to deserve its continuation?" The focus on God's presence rather than God's power is appropriately reassuring; we struggle to know and understand God's will in full awareness of God's presence among us.

Miracles

As we have seen, each model of God's relationship to the world which was developed during the eighteenth and nineteenth centuries had a distinctive definition of miracle. One model took miracles to be objectively perceivable suspensions of the causal order, another viewed miracles as internal subjective experiences, another as a matter of perception, and still another as merely external occasions for the spiritual appropriation of some truths.

An emphasis on God's presence suggests its own distinctive understanding of miracles. A miracle is a creative synchronization of the divine and the human—or the divine and the natural—wherein the presence of God is experienced and the consequences of God's presence are in some way evident. The consequences may involve a transformed life or an escape from Pharaoh's armies or a healed body. They need not be extraordinary, and they need not be universal. Their timing is extremely important. They correspond with the gift of and experience of God's presence. The active, purposeful presence of God synchronizes with the active, purposeful response of human beings in a creative way. The synchronizing is not a matter merely of perception; consequences do occur. Nor is it merely internal or psychological; the whole of a person or community of persons is involved. The significance of a miracle does not lie only in its spiritual appropriation. It is a proleptic sign of the transformation of all that is. It has both an objective and a nonobjective element: God's presence is "both hidden and revealed," as Luther liked to say.

Given the strength of presence, it is no surprise that God's presence "in, with, and under" the art of medicine, and perhaps also in seemingly extraordinary ways, can heal. Given the purposefulness of God's active presence, it is no surprise that consequences follow. The emphasis on presence removes the difficulty of reconciling natural causation and miracle. No longer must a choice be made between saying that God causes and controls everything, that God causes and controls nothing (finite causes doing all), and that God causes and controls only extraordinary breaks in the natural order. It is no longer necessary to choose between these, each of which is inadequate for the Christian faith.

The Concept of God

The particular concept of God that goes along with the model of God's revelation as presence represents God to be dynamic, noncontrolling, involved in the world, and intending a divine purpose for, in, and with it. It portrays God not as a mechanical force but as a presence that is at least personal, however more than this God may be. God is not pictured as above it all, controlling all that happens, but as an active participant, one who coexperiences the pain of the broken world, is present in that world, and celebrates each hint of truthfulness and reality found in it. To *be with* human beings is to share human reality as well as to confront, challenge, and transform it. To *be with* human beings is to be incarnate.

In this view, the emphasis is on the presence of God rather than God's power. The emphasis is on the interdependence of God and the world rather than the aseity of God. The emphasis is on the vulnerability of God rather than the divine immutability. Though God's character and purpose are consistent, the depth of God's involvement with human beings produces changes in perception and strategy. This means that though God is all-knowing in the sense of knowing all that is past and present without error, God does not literally know the future. The emphasis is also on God's inclusiveness. God is not macho but incorporates into the divine self the best of what we know as feminine and the best of what we know as masculine.[6]

The resulting picture of God involves an element of mystery, one that can never be totally penetrated by human powers of conceptualization or articulation. The picture is not of a God of absolute, self-contained, impenetrable transcendence but is more complex. Though beyond time, God is also surely in time. Though God has unchanging purposes, these get embodied in a variety of ways. Though able to get along without us humans, God is also tied so decisively to us that human beings are now called to serve God's purposes and mediate God's presence. They are cocreators and coworkers. A God who is with us is not absolutely other. God has self-identified with the humanity and finitude God loves so deeply.

Communicating the Presence of God

The process of articulating and communicating the presence of God follows upon revelation. Words usually have to be sought; they are not normally given in the revelation itself. In the main, revelation is not the reception of packaged information or knowledge from God. Whatever is gained from the presence of God is articulated only as persons touched by the divine presence reflect upon it and draw out as implications the whole range of possibilities it opens. The presence of God is the presence of Word or Logos: the divine presence is surely not antiknowledge, nor is it incapable of being expressed, but the potential for expression at first remains unactualized, because we have no ready-made categories for interpreting a presence hitherto beyond our horizon of consciousness. Words must be sought that are adequate to a new reality.[7]

The words to express and communicate the revelation may be found quickly, or the process may take a long time. Either way, words must be tested to see whether they adequately convey or mediate to others the presence of God. If they do not, a reformulation and a reinterpretation are necessary. Paul, for example, needed to write to the Corinthians because his initial formulation of the gospel had been misunderstood. Paul had to work out a new set of words that would correct the Corinthians' misinterpretation and combat their desire for "superlative" Christianity. His reformulation was possible because his earlier words were not absolute. They were instead governed by and subservient to revelation, that is, to the presence of God. His words pointed beyond themselves to an identity-forming presence of God and could be judged by their adequacy in conveying to the Corinthians the correct identity of the God whose presence had been experienced. Consequently, when Paul was misunderstood, he could hunt for more adequate words than the ones he first used. His reformulation comes down to us in 1 and 2 Corinthians.

To take another example, the disciples who lived in the presence of Jesus were so drawn to him that they left all they had to be with him. But more often than not they were confused and did not know what to make of this presence. Again and again in the Gospel accounts the disciples failed to perceive the significance of what was happening. The traditional concepts they tried to use did not fit the newly revealed embodiment of God. Not until after the resurrection, not until the event described in Acts as Pentecost, did they begin to find words that could tell others what had happened. When the church later accepted some writings as apostolic, it was because they found in them the words that had been developed and refined by the apostles to point to the Christ.

Inspiration

Our concepts of revelation and communication bring us to another reality, namely, the *ongoing* presence of God—or the Spirit—in the community's articulation of God's revealed identity. The presence of the Spirit at Pentecost opened the mouths of the apostles, but not merely at Pentecost is the Spirit active in communicating God's revelation. Whenever the people of God, formed by God's presence, hunt for words to articulate the divine presence, God's Spirit participates. The Spirit's participation is inspiration. Inspiration is not identical with revelation but is a facet of the presence of God that comes after the identity-forming disclosure and experience called revelation.

The words the Spirit helps find can be called inspired, for several reasons. First, the search for words is set in motion by the identity-forming presence of God. It is because of God's revelation that the imperative to communicate is felt. Second, God's ongoing presence accompanies the community of the faithful as they examine critically and explore, revise, and reformulate their words for expressing the revelation they have experienced. Third, any adequate words the community can frame will be transparent to the presence of God. The shaping revelation will show through, and with that the identity of God will be visible. The transparency will enable the words to mediate God's presence to others. Since ordinary words will have been stretched and pulled, the individual words may not be indispensable to the communication. But what they point to, what they are transparent to, is special and makes them inspired. They are inspired by virtue of the presence they convey. Fourth, God is present as the community endeavors to interpret the words of a previous generation in a new setting. The ways that the words are, as a result, inspired will be considered in more detail later.

Implications

The bounds of inspiration Inspiration is not limited to the books of the Bible.[8] The Spirit inspires many nonscriptural words that witness to the presence and identity of God in Christ. The more effective the words are at mediating God's presence and identity, the more likely they will be called inspired. They may issue from a somewhat less intensive search than the search that produced the New Testament and a less direct exposure to the identity-forming revelation that propelled Christianity into being, but to the degree that they are forged in the community of faith where God's Spirit is present and to the degree that they mediate to others the presence of the true God, they too must be deemed inspired.

Inspired nonscriptural sayings are subordinate to the inspired passages of the Bible in that the biblical texts passages are normative for the nonscriptural sayings. The Bible is apostolic in ways that contemporary expressions are not. The Scriptures put us into contact with the originating revelation of God that informed the apostolic writings. The inspired words of today therefore cannot overturn or contradict the apostolic witness. The Bible is normative in the sense that it offers the ultimate witness to what it means to be Christian.

The understanding of inspiration that I am recommending for postmodern culture is fully compatible with the understanding during the second century, when the church adopted as Scripture most of the writings later known as the New Testament. No strict line then separated canonical from noncanonical writings. As Hans von Campenhausen shows, works not in our canon were recommended for private use[9] and were in public use among the churches.[10] Irenaeus drew no distinction indicating that he thought the canonical books were inspired and others were not.[11] Apocalyptic writings claimed inspiration for themselves and their authors but were not on that account included in the canon.[12]

For writings to qualify for the canon, they had to meet criteria concerning age, content, and use in the churches. The criteria were a protection against the Montanists, who were producing new writings that claimed direct inspiration by the Spirit but that were often undisciplined by the apostolic witness and the community's efforts at refinement.

What happened once the Scriptures were established was that they came to discipline but did not suspend the process of articulation in the church. Sermons and the witness of one individual to another are inspired to the degree that they mediate to people the already mediated presence of God found in the Scriptures.

Inspiration as process   One value of historical criticism is to uncover the process by which inspiration occurred in the writing of the Scriptures. Historical criticism enables us to watch the people of God as they struggled to articulate and communicate the presence of God.

It allows us to discern the elements of oral tradition that antedated the texts and were incorporated into them. The purposes of the first redaction can be understood as the setting in which it was written is uncovered. And tracing the susbsequent revisions enables us to understand why the specific words and phrases were used that appear in the canonical text. All of this helps us understand the texts deeply enough to know at least the range of what they can and cannot mean, because we sense how and why the words used came to be selected. We can see that the texts encapsulate the results of a very dynamic process throughout which the inspiration of the Spirit was at work.

Though historical criticism endeavors to get behind the words as we have them in the Scriptures, the goal is not to locate more authentic levels of tradition.[13] That goal would misconstrue inspiration. Rather, the point of getting behind the words is to discover the dynamic struggle out of which they emerged. The clearer we are about the misunderstanding that Paul was trying to correct, the clearer we become about the identity and character of the presence he sought to mediate. The clearer we are about the process in which oral tradition was written down and rewritten and combined and rewritten again to form the Pentateuch, the clearer we become about the awareness of God that governed the whole process. Historical criticism helps us locate the transparency of the text by locating the dynamic nexus of revelation and context behind the words.

Infallibility and inerrancy   Words like *infallible* and *inerrant* have been used correctly referring to inspired texts, but they are dangerously misleading in our own day. By calling too much attention to the scriptural words, they draw attention away from what the words are meant to point to. They focus attention on the window rather than on what can be seen through the window.

Scriptural inerrancy lies in the Bible's not causing us to stray from the path, in its pointing readers in the right direction, toward revelation, toward the presence with us of the true God. In this sense, the term *inerrant* is appropriate on any of the four viable models discussed in chapters 2 and 3. Only if the term is understood to imply the supposed attribute of the extraordinatry accuracy of the words themselves does it become a partisan concept fitting supernaturalism alone.

Similarly, scriptural infallibility lies in the Bible's failing in its proper task of pointing us in the right direction, toward revelation, toward the presence with us of the true God. If *infallible* has to do with the way the Scriptures point beyond themselves, the concept fits more than one model of scriptural authority. Only if it is taken to call attention to a supposed attribute of the words themselves, namely, that every idea expressed by them is accurate in some literal, nonreferential way and that only words in fact employed in the Bible can convey the content intended, does it too become a partisan concept.

The terms *inerrant* and *infallible* are capable of misleading in yet another way. They obscure the need for ongoing reinterpretation. They obscure the unending search for language more adequate to the task of mediating God's presence today. They obscure the role played by the ongoing presence of God in the community of faith as that community refines its language to make it once again transparent to the presence of God. Because language changes—as anyone realizes who tried to read Old English—the words themselves are nor irreformable. Our language must be opened up to the same presence as that to which the original words witnessed.

It is true that historical criticism may also call attention to the words in such a way as to cloud their transparency. By insisting upon the historical meaning of the words, an interpreter may misunderstand a biblical passage, regarding it to be so rooted in the past as not to point beyond itself to the contemporary presence of God. Once again attention is on the window and not on what can be seen through the window. As a tool, historical criticism is neutral, in and of itself neither a good nor a bad thing. Like a hammer it may be used to break down or to build up; like a magnifying glass it may obscure or clarify the character of the text. When it deepens our understanding of the text and serves its proper task of mediating God's revelation, it builds up. When it freezes the text into the past, it obscures.

If one chooses to use *inerrant* or *infallible* or to employ the methods of historical criticism, one should do so with full awareness of the dangers and benefits of their use. In the case of historical criticism, enough is to be gained to outweigh the risks. But, in our day the misunderstanding that can be engendered by the words *inerrant* and *infallible* is more significant than whatever advantages they may offer.

Every theory of biblical authority involves an image of God's relation to the world, a view of revelation, an understanding of the relationship between revelation and the spoken or written word, and an understanding of the role of inspiration. In this chapter, I have presented one postmodern approach to these matters. I have suggested presence as the primary image of God's relation to the world and have described revelation as an identity-disclosing and an identity-forming presence of God. On the view I have developed, the spoken or written word results from attempts to understand and communicate revelation. Inspiration is God's ongoing presence with the community as it gropes for words to mediate the divine presence and identity it has experienced.

6

Biblical Usefulness, Biblical Authority

In chapter 5, I presented an image of God's relation to the world that can inform our contemporary understanding of biblical authority. I have argued that the image is at once logically extrabiblical and influenced by the identity of Christianity. It cannot claim exalted authority, as if it were the only possible or the only correct image or the one guaranteed to solve all apologetic problems. But in every theory some image forms an essential ingredient, and the proponents of any theory need to be clear about the image they employ. The theory's image—as well as its other ingredients—needs to be displayed plainly so that nothing is recommended or accepted uncritically.

The image of God's relation to the world which I have offered as meeting postmodern culture's needs should now be incorporated into a more explicit and encompassing view of the authority of the Bible. If one accepts the images of God, revelation, and inspiration that I have laid out, the question arises, Why turn to the Bible? For if, as I maintain, more than one set of words may be inspired, it must be asked why Christians have turned to the Bible and why they should continue to do so.

At least two kinds of answers can be given to this question: one functional and the other material. Neither is sufficient by itself; because the two kinds of answers complement each other, they need to be taken together.

The Functional Answer

The functional answer, in brief, is that people in the church turn to the Bible because Christians have found and continue to find it useful to do so. As 2 Tim. 3:16 says, not only are the Scriptures inspired, they are also profitable—"profitable for teaching, for reproof, for correction, and for training in righteousness." They are useful to the church as it carries out its tasks of guidance and instruction.

To explain the functional answer in more detail, it is necessary to look at the nature of authority.

Communal and contextual Authority is, first of all, communal and contextual. It is always exercised within some system or structure of an organized group of human beings. For example, the word of a chief can carry enormous authority within his tribe. It can mean death or life for those who violate the standards of the tribe and for members of other tribes when a decision is being made between war and peace. Standing on the corner of a busy intersection in an American city, however, the chief can proclaim all the words he wants and endanger no one' s life. In this setting he will be ignored, perhaps even regarded as crazy, because the authority of his office is contextual and communal and does not extend to city intersections.

Parental authority carries weight within a family, but beyond the family the authority disappears. Were parents to treat their physician the same way they do their infant children, the doctor would be perplexed and perhaps offended, because in the doctor's office a different system of authority prevails. Authority changes as the parents move from one context to another.

The queen of England may be honored and respected by an American as someone else's authority, but she has no claim on the decision making of persons outside the British Empire. (Admittedly, she may have little claim even on British citizens, but the fact that she does have some authority, however limited and symbolic, is sufficient for the point under discussion here.) Others do not look to her for direction and guidance. Authority is contextual and communal. It depends on the existence of a community of people tied together in some way. The queen of England, marooned on some deserted island, is just another human being struggling for survival. Though it may appear at first glance as if governments can impose their will on citizens, a closer look reveals that their authority depends upon the existence of a community of support, holding in common certain aspirations, attitudes, and values. Every police officer knows that there are archaic laws still on the books which are unenforceable because they are out of touch with the attitudes and values of the contemporary community. Even in a totalitarian regime, a certain degree of community support is necessary for governmental authority to be exercised. If enough people were to refuse to work, for example, the government would be powerless to restore order. In Nazi Germany, when citizens protested the euthanasia of mental patients, Hitler ordered the program halted, and it was never resumed. Any government that totally loses contact with the community ceases to be effective. Its authority crumbles.

A community also provides the context for the Bible's authority: the community of faith. In the community of faith the Bible makes its claim on persons—to be taken seriously in their decision making and to inform their sense of direction and purpose. Those outside the community of faith can respect the Bible as a document of religious significance for others, they can study it, and they may even appeal to it if they want to persuade Christians to act in a certain way (this frequently occurs in political discourse), but for them it does not, properly speaking, exercise authority. It makes no claims on their own decision making or sense of direction.

The normal sequence, therefore, is for a person to come into contact with a contemporary representative or member of the community and to have the presence of God mediated through the living voice and demeanor of this human being and then to be drawn into the fellowship that accepts and studies the Scriptures as an authority for life.[1] This normal sequence does not negate the possibility that someone may read the Bible directly and find the presence of God mediated through its pages. Even then, however, contact has been made with the community of faith, because a noncontemporary human being, a member of the community of faith in an earlier time, speaks on every page. The reader listens in on a conversation between Paul or John or Mark and the people to whom he is writing. Not until the presence of God has been mediated through the words of Mark or John or Paul do the Scriptures begin to exercise their claim or take on authority. Authority is the result rather than the presupposition of this encounter. It grows out of the functioning of the text and is the product of the text's usefulness in mediating the presence of God.

If the presence of God is arresting, transforming, and identity forming, as it was described to be in chapter 5, then the experience of God's presence effects changes, however dramatic or subtle. Recognition of the authority of the Bible is a byproduct of those sometimes complex changes. This does not mean that the acknowledgment of biblical authority is merely added on to an otherwise unaltered set of values. The changes in identity effected by God's presence lead to a quest for understanding, which in turn leads to a greater appropriation of the existential implications of God's presence and to further changes in identity and so on. The truth of the Bible is an experienced truth; existential changes need to occur in order for its truth to be recognized and acknowledged. God's presence, mediated through the community of faith, is what effects the changes.

Because authority is both a byproduct of existential change and an ingredient in it, theories of biblical authority like those discussed in chapters 2 and 3 have a limited usefulness. By selecting certain features of contemporary culture and certain aspects of the biblical message and showing how these relate to each other, the theories can endeavor to persuade contemporaries of the Bible's usefulness, but they cannot really *establish* the authority of the Bible. For that there must be contact with the community and some personal transformation. A person is not convinced of the Bible's truth before a transformative contact with the community of faith. The truth of the Bible can be established only by praxis, by living its insights in fellowship with others.

A serious deficiency of the theories outlined in chapters 2 and 3 is that they are out of date. The cultural context has changed. A second serious deficiency has now emerged. The theories have not paid enough attention to the nature and character of authority. They thus promise more than they can deliver. They promise to restore the authority of the Bible in the modern age and to preserve its authority for all who are convinced by their arguments. But because of the complexities we have been discussing, no theory can fulfill such a promise. The bitter and unproductive arguments that have developed and continue to occur between liberals and conservatives are in part the result of the theories' exaggerated promises. In short, none of these theories has had a sufficiently dynamic or sufficiently encompassing understanding of authority to be able to recognize its own limitations.

Relational Closely connected with the communal and contextual nature of authority is another feature: authority is relational. The word *authority* denominates the kind of relationship between one person and another, or between one person and a book or set of ideas, in which the "other" — the other person, the book, or the set of ideas — is acknowledged to have some claim: the other needs to be taken into account in decision making. The response to the other need not be servile obedience, but the other does demand attention. The other becomes a point of reference or orientation, that to which a person turns without a new justification on each and every occasion. Because authority is relational, it develops over time and involves an element of trust and trustworthiness.

To say that authority is relational is to reject as incomplete two other interpretations of it, both commonly asserted. Of these, the first regards authority as created by an arbitrary choice. On this view, persons give or grant authority to the other. Authority is constituted by their decision to allow the other to influence their lives. This view pulls authority out of the relationship and lodges it with the one over whom authority is exercised.

Many things may be said in behalf of this view. For example, it correctly emphasizes that the person over whom authority is exercised participates in the authority relationship. As a participant, the person may reject some or all of the claims being made and needs to take ownership for whatever claims are acknowledged. Because there is a volitional aspect to the authority relationship, obedience to a superior does not relieve the person of responsibility. Still, authority is not some creation of the participant's. The claims authority makes are an aspect of the relationship. Though the participant may indeed acknowledge or reject any one of the claims, it does not follow that the authority reflected in the claims is itself constituted by the volition of the person involved in the authority relationship. Think of parental authority. Authority is present in any parent-child relationship (assuming, of course, that the word *parent* means more than merely biological paternity or maternity and includes rearing). Parents make claims on the decision making of their children and become points of reference that help their children orient their lives. Parental authority exists for a child even before there is awareness that it exists, and certainly before the child consciously affirms its validity. The child, obviously, had no choice of parents and, only a little less obviously, no choice about entering the authority relationship with them. Though never passive—not even before adolescence, when a relatively more conscious affirmation or rejection occurs— the child exercises volitional involvement within the authority relationship. Rebellion, when it occurs, is directed against the child's parents and what they stand for, not against some other parents or some other set of values. Even in rebellion the child is shaped by the parental claim, albeit in a somewhat negative manner and with consequences quite different from those that grow out of greater harmony and acceptance.

Think too of governmental authority. Unless one has immigrated by conscious choice, citizenship makes claims that are not of one's own creation. The citizen does not give authority to the government; its authority accompanies citizenship, as a part of the relationship between citizen and homeland.

The analogy to membership in the Christian community is clearest in the case of those baptized as infants and nurtured within the community of faith. But even in the case of adult baptism the claim of the Christ is present before it is acknowledged. Moreover, acceptance of Christ's authority yields a range of secondary claims one is hardly aware of beforehand. A man and woman who marry do not really know all they are affirming when they enter into a permanent relationship. More is involved than can be known in advance and explicitly affirmed. The same is true for a person entering into relationship with God in Christ.

The point is this: authority is not *constituted* by free choice. Our acknowledgement of authority is an important aspect of the authority relationship, but it does not create either the relationship or the claims made within the relationship.

109

The second interpretation to be rejected as incomplete regards authority as a possession or attribute. This interpretation is inspired by the linguistic peculiarity that we say someone or something *"has* authority." The inference is drawn that a person or thing can possess authority whether or not anyone acknowledges it. The element of truth in this approach is that the claims of an authority relationship precede our acknowledgement of their validity and, in any case, operate independently of any acknowledgment we may make. So long as we live within a particular community (family, nation, whatever), claims are made upon us whether we accede to them or not. Because the claims made in an authority relationship are to some extent beyond our control, the other seems to "possess" authority.

But we must recall that authority is always exercised within a community. Were authority possessed, it could be transferred outside the community and any claims made by the queen of England on the citizens of another country would have to be accepted as legitimate. But, as we have already noticed, this is not the way authority works. To be sure, power may be wielded beyond the realm of legitimate authority, but authority entails a relationship different from that of power, and the authority relationship has a communal base. To portray authority as a possession or attribute is thus to offer an incomplete description.

The Bible does not possess authority, nor is its authority based on some attribute that makes it utterly distinctive and absolutely different from every other writing. Its authority does not depend on its inspiration, in the sense that it would if the Bible were alone inspired, nor does biblical authority depend on Scripture's being uniquely error-free. Indeed, the Bible does not possess authority at all, except in the context of community and relationship.

Yet, someone may ask, are not all human beings children of God? If the God of the Bible is the one true God, does not the Bible, which witnesses to this God, make claims on all human beings irrespective of whether they acknowledge its claim or not? The first thing to say in response is that from faith's perspective the Bible ought to exercise its claim on all human beings but in fact does not, because sin has broken the God-human relationship. Its authority resumes only as the relationship is restored by the Spirit who works through the message of grace proclaimed by human beings belonging to the community. The second is that the imprint of the Creator is still present in the lives of human beings outside the community of faith and is recognizable to the eyes of faith in somewhat the same way that light is reflected from broken glass. The assertion that all are the children of God is made by those *in* the community of faith with respect to those living apart from community with God. It may not be evident to those beyond the community's boundaries. Therefore the Bible can make no effective claim on those outside the community and in fact has no genuine authority for them.

Authority is neither only a matter of choice nor only a possession of the other. It is a kind of relationship, one that develops over time in the context of community. It is the kind of relationship in which the other exercises a claim on the thinking and behavior of the participant.

Tacit   Authority is also tacit.[2] It comes into being as a byproduct of life lived in community. (Note that I am here discussing authority and how it comes into play, not how a theory or understanding of authority develops.) It is established not consciously and deliberately but implicitly as attention is focused on the tasks of the community. In a crisis or in some other moment of reflection, the results of the authority-establishing process are recognized and acknowledged, and then the patterns of authority can be specified but the recognition and acknowledgment do not themselves establish the authority. An authority relationship has already developed.

Consider a task-oriented committee.[3] By virtue of appointment or election one person chairs the meetings and would seem to possess authority. Yet the appearance of possessing authority may be deceiving. Imagine that as the committee addresses its task it encounters an almost intractable problem. After the committee conducts an extended discussion a member offers a breakthrough suggestion. With some relief and a good deal of appreciation, the rest of the committee endorses the member's proposal. The committee moves on to confront other problems. If the same member is consistently resourceful in coming up with proposals to solve them, that member, whether chairperson or not, will become an authority for the group. An authority relationship will develop, and when the committee confronts its next obstacle someone will turn to the resourceful person and ask, "What do you think we should do?" Committee members will be reluctant to defy the person's advice. His or her words will have a claim upon the committee and will need to be taken seriously, however much they may also be tested and modified by subsequent discussion. Functional authority is a product of insight and wisdom and usefulness to the task at hand. Functional authority may or may not coincide with designated authority. The chairperson may or may not become the functional authority for the committee. It is therefore inappropriate to consider authority as essentially a possession. Functional authority develops over time and is far more effective than designated authority. Though it too may be lost, it alone is genuine.

To say that authority formation is tacit is to acknowledge that the committee members were not intentionally elevating the status of their colleague, nor were they even thinking in terms of choosing an authority. The authority relationship came into being as the group attended to its task and to the obstacles encountered in fulfilling its responsibility. The authority relationship was a byproduct of the committee's interaction. If asked to reflect, members might acknowledge that a pattern of authority had emerged. Their admission would not change the functional reality, but with it the authority relationship would cease to be tacit; it would be acknowledged and could be specified.

Now extend the example another step. Assume a new committee member enters the group. This person soon senses what is going on and, after testing the trustworthiness and competence of the person in authority, either shares the judgment of the other members or opposes it. If the new member joins the consensus, things will go smoothly, though numerous details will need to be discussed and many problems worked out along the way. If the new member rejects the group's opinion, there may be a crisis in the dynamics of the group which will need to be resolved. The committee may struggle along with rival authorities, the new member may emerge as a leader, the new member may leave, or there may be some other outcome. All of this will happen because "a member's role is worked out jointly by the person and the group."[4]

The church first considered the writings we now call the New Testament valuable because they spoke to the problems at hand, problems such as schism in Corinth, Judaizers in Galatia, the understanding of Christian identity after the destruction of the temple, and the appropriate degree of strictness or laxity in the congregations addressed by Matthew. Other congregations who faced similar problems copied and circulated the writings. Still others found in them a useful witness to apostolic preaching and teaching as clarity in such matters became important in the face of Gnostic appeals to esoteric traditions. In short, documents were found to be useful as congregations addressed themselves to the tasks of the church: preaching, teaching, worshiping, counseling, and proclaiming and embodying the kingdom of God. Except for Marcion, no one intended to create a new Scripture. Attention was rather on the tasks at hand, for which the writings provided a helpful resource. Over time and through the church's use of the texts, an authority relationship gradually emerged. When, in the last half of the second century, it seemed important for the church to have a canon of writings, Irenaeus and other church leaders identified those with which an authority relationship had already developed, writings that were already widely used among the congregations of the church. Contrary to Marcion's recommendation, the writings selected for the canon included the Septuagint, the Greek translation of the Hebrew Scriptures that later came to be called the Old Testament.

In the church a crisis prompted the acknowledgment and specification of the authority that had already developed tacitly. Marcion precipitated the crisis. In many ways like someone joining a committee, he entered the church in the 140s. Soon he began recommending that the church narrow its attention to a fairly short list of books, including an edited version of Luke, some Pauline epistles, and no Septuagint. Because Marcion's canon seemed inconsistent with customary use and the fullness of the church's identity, the church responded by affirming the usefulness of the Old Testament and of a more inclusive list of specifically Christian writings, which became the New Testament. Though theologians and leaders offered their reasons, no one in the church appointed these writings to authority. By consensus the church acknowledged an already existing authority relationship that had evolved gradually over decades. The church did not elevate the writings to authority, for they were writings that had already come to have a claim on the loyalty and identity of Christians.

One answer, then, to the question, Why turn to the Bible? is that the church has used the books over the centuries, recognizing their insight, their wisdom, and their usefulness as resources for accomplishing the church's proper tasks: evangelism, teaching, healing, worship, and so on. Having found them useful, the church has continued to turn to them for guidance whenever new problems have been encountered. After generations and centuries of finding them useful, the church has become more and more reluctant to ignore their claim or go against what they say. The writings have therefore exercised authority in the Christian community, making claims on the members, influencing their decision making, and informing the church's sense of purpose and direction.

The functional authority of biblical documents is not static. Though each generation in the church inherits the advice to turn to the Scriptures for help and though the accumulated weight of tradition reinforces and strengthens the Bible's claim upon us, the usefulness of the biblical documents needs constantly to be confirmed anew. In one sense, their usefulness needs to be rediscovered by each generation, because the recommendation of the previous generation makes the documents but a designated authority. Mere designation gives them little claim until it is confirmed by a developing functional authority. A genuine authority relationship emerges only through use.

The functional answer, by the way, goes a long way even toward explaining the influence of the Scriptures in certain fundamentalist churches and sects. The influence exerted by the Scriptures in the lives of persons in these congregations does not depend on the particular theory of authority that the congregations accept—as some partisans would claim—but depends instead upon the actual use of the Bible. The Bible is studied, discussed, and applied to people's lives in worship services, prayer groups, and evening study groups. Through extensive use the Bible exerts influence no matter what theory of its authority is embraced.

Exalted statements about the authority of the Bible may actually be counterproductive. If one has been told to expect something of Scripture and finds in using the Bible that one's expectation is unmet, the disillusionment can be serious. It can stifle an appropriate appreciation of the biblical documents' trustworthiness. Modest promises are the more prudent: the presence of God mediated by the Scriptures will, in any case, make its own claims.

No particular theory is necessary in order for functional authority to develop. A recommendation to use the Scriptures is enough. "We have found them useful in the past, why not try them as you participate in the life of this community of faith and attend to Christian living?" The best a theory can do is give some hints about how to use the Scriptures without violating their integrity and about how to make connections between certain scriptural features and features of contemporary life. Unfortunately, most theories—probably including my own—are insufficiently encompassing to allow the Bible to be all that it is and all that it may become in the life of the church. Such is the rich diversity the Bible has to offer. And such is the rich variety of use one finds in the church universal.

The Material Answer

The second answer to the question, Why turn to the Bible? is a material one. After the functional answer is given, the question still remains why the biblical books have turned out to be so useful. What do they offer that keeps the church from being disappointed each time it tests the inherited tradition? The material answer addresses the question by underscoring the interlocking observations that the Bible mediates the presence of God and that it provides the language of faith.

Capacity to mediate   Christians turn to the Bible because its writings have the capacity to mediate the identity-forming presence of God. In a metaphor, the Scriptures are transparent: revelation shows through the Bible's words. The words of Scripture point beyond themselves to the revelation that gave rise to them in the first place. When used properly in the context of Christian community, the words communicate to readers and listeners the identity-forming presence of God. They mediate to the present generation the revelation that shaped the identity of the Christian community.

The Christian community did not decide to become a community. (In fact, I wonder whether a genuine community of any depth can be created by decision, in any case.) It was not formed as a chess club would be, with individuals of similar interests deciding to associate with one another for mutual benefit and enjoyment. As Paul's First Letter to the Corinthians argues convincingly, the church is marked by startling diversity yet held together by a common call and a common bond of love. A divine call holds together an otherwise nonuniform group of people. Moreover, the locus of authority is different from what it is in a strictly voluntary association. A chess club may organize itself and write a constitution that takes on a certain degree of authority, but ultimate authority is retained by the membership. They can change or even abandon the constitution at will; the club has more authority than the document it creates. Unlike a chess club, the Christian church was *called* into being. A series of encounters with the presence of God, extending at least from Abraham through Pentecost, generated its call. What created and defined the called community—revelation—has higher authority than the community itself. Unlike a chess club, which can transform itself into a bridge club and alter its constitution accordingly, the church cannot alter its calling, though it may articulate and embody its calling in different ways from age to age and from culture to culture. Whatever mediates the call partakes of the call's authority. Thus, because the Scriptures witness to the identity-forming revelation on which the church is built, they have a claim upon the church. They partake of the authority that called the church into being. Scripture's claim on the church may be supplemented and interpreted but never displaced, if the church is not to cease to be the church, in a break of continuity with its original call. Even though the messages that mediate the identity-forming revelation can be found elsewhere—for example, in the worship life and traditions of the community of faith or even in other writings produced by the church—the Scriptures remain the normative form for expressing the revelation. Other expressions are interpreted in terms of the scriptural writings and not vice versa.

Earlier in this chapter I gave reasons for not viewing authority as constituted solely by personal volition. I can now give another. Within a called community the documents that mediate the originating revelation have a claim upon members independent of the members' own commitments and personal interests. Persons encounter that claim the moment they are in contact with the community. It antedates the normative documents but is mediated through them; it influences and informs the identity of the community and is not produced by the community's own makeup or its peculiar priorities or its contemporary decisions.

Language of faith   The material answer to the question, Why turn to the Bible? has a second, and interlocking, component in the observation that the Scriptures provide the language of faith. Up to this point I have emphasized the movement from God's presence to the words embodying God's presence, the movement from experience to the articulation and communication of the experience. If we were to stop there, however, the character of human existence and the character of life in the community of faith would be oversimplified to the point of distortion, because experience never occurs in a vacuum. No human being approaches life with a clean slate, empty of all categories, lacking any image of reality. If one could trace the history of the community of faith back to its very beginning, whenever that was, one would find human beings who carried with them a certain "language"—a linguistic structure and vocabulary that embodied a particular way of perceiving their life in the world. What they encountered in revelation was an experience of God's presence that their language did not fit. Their language needed to be stretched and adopted to accommodate and communicate the insights their new experience brought.[5] Each subsequent new experience required further stretchings and adaptations until a language was developed that communicated God's presence and the identity of the community of faith with some adequacy. The Bible contains the language that the community of faith arrived at.

Neither do members of today's community of faith choose their vocabulary or develop it from scratch. They are schooled in the existing language of the community, which is drawn from the Scriptures. By conferring on the community its normative language, the Scriptures exercise significant authority, for in effect they define reality for members of the community. New experiences are interpreted by reference to scriptural language, and the landscape of the world is defined by this language. Alterations in the language occur only after the strict consideration of significant dissonances between the community's experience and the language it has inherited. More often than not new experiences do not require linguistic alterations; they simply prompt the community to reappropriate neglected dimensions of the language provided by the Scriptures.

We do well to remind ourselves that events and experiences are never entirely prelinguistic. Experiences bring together language and an occasioning occurrence. Someone once told me how the East Coast blackout of November 1965 was an event for him. He had been reading about the energy crisis, but the reading had made no strong impression on him. Then he experienced the blackout, and the energy crisis became a part of his world. The blackout without the reading—without the conceptual framework, without the language of crisis—would have been a quickly forgotten, insignificant inconvenience. But with the language it became an event, a perception-altering experience. The experience to which the evangelicalist theory discussed in chapter 2 appeals is thus not neutral but already in part the product of the biblical language it is believed to validate.

In the life of a Christian the language of faith combines with occasioning occurrences to create events and experiences to give meaning and value and color to an otherwise quite forgettable and monotonous stream of happenings. The language of faith is thus not neutral: it is a constitutive force in the perceptual world of the believer and the community of which the believer is a part. The language of the Bible as it informs the language of the community distinguishes the world of the Christian from the worlds of other religions and other philosophies but in such a way as to encompass much that is true in other visions.

Antonius Gunneweg and Walter Schmithals observe in the book *Authority* that

> if one inquires as to the ultimate basis of *auctoritas*,
> the etymology provides a clue. *Auctoritas* is
> connected with *augere* = "to grow, to increase." The
> *auctor* is augmenter and master, source and author,
> begetter, teacher, advocate. Actually, genuine
> authority is grounded in the obvious fact that every
> man must learn, for the sake of his life; in order to
> become a man, every man needs other men as
> augmenters or authors of his own life.[6]

The Bible has authority because it "goes ahead" of the community. Its language is sufficiently profound to give greater and greater depth to the experienced reality of God's presence. It is sufficiently diverse and unified and profound not to be outgrown. Its authority is retained even as the believer and the community mature in their faith and grow in their understanding of reality.

One reason the Bible can function as an authority in the church is that its contents elicit a sense of awe. Richard Sennett points out that in general a person in authority elicits a sense of awe or fear or dread. The awe or fear or dread derives in part from the strength, ability, and capacity for superior judgment exhibited by the one in authority. And it derives in part from the presence of the leader who can forge discipline and change behavior through reference to a higher standard. The Bible exhibits qualities similar to those Sennett finds in persons who exercise authority. It inspires awe, in part by exhibiting a superior understanding of God. It knows more than believers do; thus it inspires awe and invites investigation. It changes behavior by sketching a higher path and challenging the reader or hearer to follow. And it conveys a presence. Something of the mystery of election by the sovereign God pervades the Old Testament to give it the power to cause a sense of awe. Something of the charisma of Christ pervades the New Testament to extend this power. Through its pages the transcendent One is encountered as a benevolent, strong, awe-inspiring presence. The Bible thus deserves reexamination and study. In the interaction of Bible and community the community is convinced of the usefulness of Scripture.

Moreover, any individual's perception of the Bible remains partial. The language that has been appropriated is the language that has been enlivened by experience and that has so informed and highlighted occurrences as to transform them into events. Not unless generations of experience were assimilated into one life would the language of the Bible be exhausted and surpassed. Without that, Scripture remains an instrument of growth and maturation, the effective source and norm for the life and theology of the community.

The Bible mediates the identity-forming experiences of revelation. The Bible provides the language of faith. These two interlocking affirmations provide the material answer to the question, Why turn to the Bible?

Consequences

From the material answer several consequences follow.

Continuity One consequence of the kind of stable but not stagnant material relevance that the Scriptures have is that they are the indispensable agent of continuity in the church. They mediate the identity-forming revelation that called the church into being, and they provide the language of faith. They do this for the entire diverse church, in different cultures and in different ages. Worship mediates revelation and informs the language of faith, as do preaching and evangelism as well as the teachings and doctrines, and even the art and architecture, of the church. But all these constituents of the church's life change too much or change too little to provide continuity. When they change too much they lose the richness of the originating revelation and the language of faith. When they change too little they petrify into formalism and lose touch with present realities. The Scriptures revitalize by bridging the centuries and bringing the church into contact with the originating vision and rich language of the formative period. Encounter with the Scriptures re-focuses the identity of the church as a called community.

Scripture has not always been at the center of the community of faith. The people of Israel flourished for a thousand years or more without written Scriptures, and the church functioned for about 150 years without a religiously authoritative collection of writings reflecting its unique post-Easter language. (It did, of course, have the Septuagint.) Indeed, even when writings were available, the oral word was at first preferred.[8] It is possible for the language of faith to be the spoken word, but only when the original words are memorized and handed down exactly as delivered. The richer and more diverse what is handed down, the less possible oral transmission is. And the more international the religious movement, the more the difficulties grow. Given the geographical extent of the church and the wealth of material Christians want to preserve, the Scriptures are now functionally indispensable to the community: the alternative is impoverishment.

Because the language and experience of the church are so rich, continuity cannot be guaranteed by a single set of propositions or by a single liturgical practice. Continuity is rediscovered as the language of the Scriptures is reappropriated amid the involvements of the present.

Normativity Another consequence of the material answer is that the Scriptures are normative. By mediating the identity-forming presence of God and by providing the language of faith, the Scriptures being members of the church into contact with God's claim upon their lives. The Scriptures communicate and amplify the call that constitutes and reconstitutes the Christian community. The life and practice and teachings of the church are worked out under the guidance of the Scriptures.

More important than affirming *that* the Scriptures are normative, however, is specifying *how* they are normative. In the first place, they do not lord it over the church. They are instead servants of revelation — that is, servants both of God's presence and of the human discovery of that presence, its claims, and its implications. The authority of the Scriptures is a derived authority, one exercised vicariously on behalf of God in revelation. Just as God's presence was incarnate in the humanity of Jesus the Christ and just as God there exhibited divine strength through vulnerability and brokenness, so it is with the Scriptures. They are no higher than their master. Their witness is also an incarnate witness, fully embodied in the individuality of the various writers and fully immersed in the shape of the communities they rep-

119

resent and address, reflecting candidly the horizons of their own historical and cultural context. One should not expect them to offer self-evident credentials. One should not expect them to be without inaccuracies and inconsistencies in historical detail. One should not expect their every assumption to be in harmony with the science of a later age. The Scriptures are normative in their capacity to serve and to mediate revelation, in their capacity to illumine and deepen the human experience of God's presence. They do not have a prescription for every problem, an answer to every question, or a blueprint for every future development. The church is not called to serve but to be served by the Bible.

It follows that using the Scriptures to intimidate rather than to give life is inappropriate in the church, as is using the Scriptures merely to buttress and enhance the prestige of church leaders and officials. The God portrayed in the Scriptures does not manipulate but takes the greatest risks and goes to the furthest extreme—loss of the Son—to enlist us as companions and partners in the regeneration of the world. God's agenda for human beings is challenging, and the responsibility God bestows on human beings is awesome and frightening, but intimidation is missing. The exercise of scriptural authority must be congruent with the exercise of God's authority: its role is one of life-giving service.

In the second place, the Scriptures are normative in more than one way. Different pasts of Scripture may have differing kinds and degrees of authority, depending on the issue and circumstances facing the community. For instance, the witness of the Scriptures is both kerygmatic and confessional.

The words of the Scripture function kerygmatically when they convey a message from God to human beings. God's gracious deeds, God's mercy and favor are announced and proclaimed. As is clear from previous discussions, the exact formulation of God's message may not have come from God. It may be God's Word without being literally God's own speech.

The words of Scripture function confessionally when they embody or recommend a specific form of human response to God's favor and activity. The character, reflective identity, and responsibilities of human beings in response to God are articulated in confessional language. Worship, praise, and gratitude are expressed, and the shape of faithful living is designated. Embodied in this language are the ethics of the community, their priorities and structure. In Deuteronomy 5, for example, the reminder that "the Lord God made a covenant with us in Horeb" is kerygmatic; the commandments that follow are confessional.

The kerygmatic and the confessional are correlative. Any specific proclamation implies an analogous form of confession. One cannot with integrity proclaim a gospel of freedom and a policy of tyranny. Again and again the prophets remind Israel of this correlation. In Jer. 2:7, for example, we read,

> And I brought you into a plentiful land
> to enjoy its fruits and its good things.
> But when you came in you defiled my land,
> and made my heritage an abomination.

And the correlation carries over into the New Testament. In 1 John 4:16, 20, we find, "God is love. . . . If any one says, 'I love God,' and hates his brother, he is a liar." Conversely, each form of confession assumes a particular message from God as its authorization. Paul's kerygmatic message is slightly different from Luke's or John's or Mark's; the message of the Deuteronomic historian is slightly different from that of the Jahwist in the Pentateuch. No pure kerygma occurs in the Scriptures. There are no nonincarnate words of God, none that are not entangled in the confessional perceptions of the speakers or authors.

Owing to the correlative character of the confessional and the kerygmatic, the words and statements of Scripture should not be divided into separate, isolated categories. Some may be more clearly kerygmatic, others more obviously confessional, but the kerygmatic should be seen in the confessional and the confessional in the kerygmatic. If it were not for this, it would be possible to discount scriptural passages that seem out-of-date. But every passage is to be taken seriously, even if distinctions can be drawn between portions of the Bible with regard to their character and degree of authority.

The significance of the distinction between the kerygmatic and the confessional lies in the acknowledgment that the Scriptures may be normative in more than one way. The claim upon the hearer made by the kerygmatic is direct and existential. It creates and deepens the personal relationship between God and the hearers.[9] Though we may compare one kerygmatic statement with another and in our setting find one more transparent than another, ultimately we humans have no vantage from which to assess the kerygma's fidelity to God. We may assess the transparency of the words used, but if God is not gracious and caring, then the Scriptures are built upon error or deception and no amount of adjustment will make any difference one way or another. The kerygmatic cannot be compromised without destroying its character. When the authors and signers of the Barmen Declaration perceived Nazi policies and Nazi propaganda to be revising the kerygma, they could do

121

nothing but say no and affirm again the lordship of Jesus and the limitations of loyalty to race, state, and Führer.[10]

The claims made by the confessional are less direct and less immediate, except insofar as they carry with them elements of the kerygmatic. The confessional is paradigmatic in the sense of illustrating more or less appropriate ways to embody the kerygmatic. One finds in the Scriptures both confessional embodiments and evaluations of them. One finds alterations and replacements. The confessional is so contextual, so much a product of the interaction of kerygma and context, that the claim of any particular confessional response must be reevaluated by each generation. It must be tested by reference both to the kerygmatic and to the present setting. Is the form of confession as it occurred at an earlier time and another place an appropriate embodiment for this time and place? Is it transparent to revelation and correlative to the character and identity of the God-for-us?

The Bible itself records how the generations struggled in evaluating the confessional material of previous generations. Changes occurred. The loose tribal confederation of the judges gave way to the monarchy. The people of faith moved from a nomadic to an agricultural to an urban existence, and adjustments were necessary. Guidelines for agricultural life that were worked out in response to the exodus and the conquest needed revision to fit the commercial patterns of a later age. The prophets, the Pharisees, Jesus, and the apostles were all in one way or another involved in revising the community's confessional response.

Appropriate confessional responses are derived from the kerygmatic. Exodus 20, for example, begins, "I am the Lord your God, who brought you out of the land of Egypt, out of the house of bondage" (Exod. 20:2). All the behavioral guidelines listed in Exodus 20–23 follow from this kerygmatic beginning. Occasionally the connection is made explicit: "You shall not wrong a stranger or oppress him, for you were strangers in the land of Egypt" (Exod. 22:21). Paul's Epistle to the Romans follows a similar pattern, with eleven chapters devoted to announcing what God has done, and then, after a therefore (Rom. 12:1), chapters 12 through 16 devoted to outlining the kind of behavior appropriate to a community built on what God has done. Because the claims of the confessional are correlative to the kerygmatic, they are slightly more indirect and contextual. And because they are more indirect and contextual, a variety of confessional responses have been preserved in the Bible, along with critiques of earlier embodiments and records of the reasons for making revisions and changes. Here is a valuable set of resources for the contemporary community of faith as it assesses its confessional response to the kerygmatic so that it may be appropriate to its time and setting.

In the third place, the Scriptures may be in part superseded by later decisions and insights. The Scriptures cannot be replaced or dispensed with. What is more, the rejection of Montanism in the ancient church means that no new revelations can alter the kerygmatic proclamation of the Scriptures. The kerygmatic function of the Scriptures cannot be superseded or circumvented. Even the predominantly confessional content of the Bible can never be ignored; it always needs to be taken seriously by the Christian community. It remains possible, however, for a particular confessional recommendation to be rendered out-of-date by historical circumstance or perceived in retrospect. to be an incomplete response to the message it was seeking to embody. The language of faith is normative but not coercive: it is malleable enough to be refashioned as the ongoing work of the Spirit in the community brings deeper insight into the implications the originating revelation has for life in our own time.

There are biblical examples of the community's reconsideration of Scripture's confessional recommendations. The New Testament community decided the ceremonial commands of the Pentateuch were not binding on Christians of gentile background. After the destruction of the temple in 70 C.E. the New Testament community felt no need to rebuild it according to the specifications given to Solomon. Nor did they feel a need to participate in the revolt aimed at securing independence from Rome, despite the divine promise to Abraham that his descendants would be a "great nation" and to David that his descendants would occupy the throne of Israel forever, and despite their own claim to be Abraham's and David's descendants.

There are also postbiblical examples. Nowhere in Scripture is slavery forbidden. But the character of the revelation mediated by the Bible points to a community of faith in which the divisiveness of slavery and its dehumanizing effects—at least as it came to be practiced in modern times—are inappropriate. Thus some Christians in the Middle Ages and again in the nineteenth century were led to repudiate slavery. Gradually their opposition has come to prevail. The community's confessional response has been altered to correspond with a deeper perception of the implications of the kerygmatic message of the Scriptures. The kerygmatic has not been superseded, but its earliest confessional embodiment has been, and this is as it should be.

Regarding women, we encounter conflicting testimony in the Bible. In the Gospel of John, the Samaritan woman at the well is the paradigmatic disciple, doing what Nicodemus did not.[11] In Luke-Acts, women play key roles equal to or even more important than those filled by males. In every account of the empty tomb, women are credited with

123

the discovery. Paul, however, seems cautious, affirming the general principle that "there is neither male nor female; for you are all one in Christ Jesus" (Gal. 3:28) but recommending to the Corinthians a prudent observance of traditional patterns regarding head covering and public speaking (1 Cor. 11:10; 14:34). And the pastoral epistles quite explicitly subordinate women to men. Because of the diversity in biblical testimony it is impossible to claim that the Scriptures prohibit women from leadership roles. The minimum requirement the Christian community must meet is to search diligently to understand revelation and its implications, to seek the most appropriate confessional embodiment possible in the present. The church may choose from conflicting confessional testimony in the Bible, but no direct scriptural mandate can be claimed for the choice. Rather, the choice must be defended by appeal to the kerygma: by sifting the confessional options available in the scriptures and tracing out their impact if followed in the present, and by assessing whether an adoption today of the various options would be consistent with the confessional implications of the Christian kerygma. My own conclusion would endorse the full and equal participation of women in the leadership of the Christian community. The reason is not that individual rights and individual autonomy are important. To argue on that ground would be to adopt the values of modern culture. I would rest my conclusion on four considerations. (1) Paul's rejection of distinctions in Galatians is more general and more authoritative for us than his advice to the Corinthians, hedged as the advice is by hesitation and qualifications. His reasons for asking women to keep silent no longer apply. (2) The witness of John and of Luke-Acts is supportive. (3) There seems to be nothing in the kerygmatic function of the Scriptures that would lead one to distinguish between men and women in the church. What occurred in the practice of the early church is contextual and cultural rather than integral to the identity and continuity of the church. To exclude women from leadership in the church is to confuse the confessional with the kerygmatic. (4) The effect of excluding women from leadership is to impoverish the church in our day and to endorse cultural forces that diminish their dignity. My four considerations may go beyond the Scriptures, but they do not ignore the witness of the Scriptures.[12]

Thus a specific aspect of the Scriptures can be superseded without rejecting or ignoring the normative character of the Scriptures in the life of the church. A revelation mediated to the community by the Scriptures may today warrant a confessional response that diverges from the one encountered in the pages of Scripture. Paradoxically, the authoritative witness of Scripture calls for the community to go beyond the Scriptures, that is, beyond the confessional embodiments recorded there. For the Scriptures themselves report how the confessional outlook of the Bible has at times been reconsidered. The Scriptures therefore point to conditions under which a reconsideration may occur again. Even the Bible does not capture God's revelation in counsels that can remain unchanged forever.

One fact that needs emphasis is that when the community of faith decides to go beyond specific scriptural mandates, it need not be merely endorsing contemporary culture or caving in to the pressures of the moment. Those who think that every change in Christian values is a deplorable accommodation to extra-Christian society have misunderstood the changes. In opposing exposure of infants and the practice of slavery and in trying to stop the escalation of the nuclear-arms race, the community of faith has been ahead of popular sentiment. It has influenced and humanized society rather than caving in to societal pressure. The impetus to go beyond the Scriptures is sparked by fidelity to the kerygmatic witness of the Scriptures rather than by an uncritical desire to keep up with the times and to change the faith in order to accommodate to contemporary society. Historically the integrity of the church has been lost more often by failing to change when change was warranted than by changing too much or too quickly. The cultural context may provide the occasion but cannot provide the justification for repudiating specific confessional recommendations of the Bible.

We have seen that the authority of the Scriptures is a derived authority. The Scriptures are useful for communicating God's presence and identity. Their task is to point beyond themselves and enable the community of faith to respond directly to God. They are not to *be* served but to serve a task and a relationship.

Interlocking features   The material answer offers two interlocking observations: that the Bible mediates the presence of God, and that the Bible provides the language of faith. The mediation of the presence of God and the provision of the language of faith are interlocking features of the Bible. If Scripture did not mediate the presence of God, it would afford no basis upon which to evaluate and alter the language of faith. If it did not provide the language of faith, its words would have no distinctive authority. The experiences underlying the Bible would be regarded as so much more valuable than the biblical words that the specific content of the Scriptures could be relativized as but one of innumerable expressions of experience, no more valid or valuable than many another expression.

In contrast to the functional answer, the material answer is incapable of spanning the various images of God's relation to the world.

125

In fact, any material reason anyone gives for turning to the Bible will build on one image of revelation rather than another. The material reason I give is no exception: it is shaped by the images I identified in chapter 5. Had I portrayed revelation as primarily the communication of supernatural information, for example, I would have had to work out a very different material reason for turning to Scripture. The material answer is not theologically neutral in the same way as the functional answer.[13]

Diversity   A final consequence of the material answer is a moral of tolerance. Once we see that the material answer of this chapter presupposes an extrabiblical decision regarding the character of revelation—and that any material reason anyone can give for turning to Scripture presupposes a comparable extrabiblical decision—we will be less likely to think that only one conception of revelation and only one theory of scriptural authority can be acceptable within the Christian church. No one is surprised that some may think of the Christ as primarily a revealer, others as primarily a forgiver, and still others as primarily a reconciler, yet that all may remain within the church. It should be no more surprising that some may picture revelation as the communication of information, others as acts of God, and still others as God's presence—each group having its own notion of scriptural authority as a result—without dividing the church. There may be better and worse views, but there is no one biblically mandated view of the dynamics of revelation and the status of the Scriptures.

What I explore and offer here is *a* view. Neither it nor any other view can guarantee the Bible a hearing or save the church from the responsibility of rethinking its identity in every age. My view cannot claim to be the only possible approach even for this age, because a diversity of cultures persist today—some premodern, others modern, and still others postmodern. Nor can I claim that my view is the only one that will permit the gospel to be heard. All I can claim is that it removes stumbling blocks that interfere with the message of the Scriptures, that it provides a more dynamic and useful understanding of the Bible's claims on us in postmodern times, and that it offers a comprehensive portrait of how things can work when the church responds appropriately to the Scriptures, to their normative and yet noncoercive authority.

A Look Back

How does my answer to the question, Why turn to the Bible? relate to the theories outlined in chapters 2 and 3? My emphasis on the communal and contextual character of biblical authority acknowledges insights found also in the ecclesial developmentalist approach, for which the Bible belong's to the community of faith, is rooted in that community, and exercises its authority there. Ecclesial developmentalism uses its insights to pursue topics and support conclusions that are not, however, germane to postmodern life. It counters the bias of modern culture against tradition with arguments concerning the historicity of the biblical documents. Moreover, the ecclesial developmentalist approach tends to regard the Scriptures, as well as postbiblical theological language, as expressive. It is therefore far less explicit than I have tried to be about the constitutive role played by the language of faith.

The communal and contextual character of scriptural authority is largely rejected by supernaturalism and overlooked by evangelicalism. If evangelicalism explored the implications of the ecclesial setting in which inner, awakening experiences occur, it would perhaps recognize the importance of community and context, but its apologetic interests keep its focus instead on the self-authenticating character of the individual's inner experience. Implicit within the evangelicalist approach is a recognition of the relational character of authority, but this too is usually not explicated. Instead, the focus settles on the volitional and the idea that a Christian grants authority to the Scriptures on the basis of an inner experience.

Supernaturalism looking in the other direction, considers authority a possession or attribute of the document itself. It seeks objective evidence to support its assertion that the Scriptures are distinctive and unique, and it takes authority to be a corollary of the kind of uniqueness it finds in the Bible.

None of the positions mentioned in chapters 2 and 3 devote much attention to the tacit character of authority, in part because they feel that the rest of Christian teaching will be credible only if the authority of the Bible is acknowledged first. This is natural in addressing the challenge of modern culture. But cultural developments have now pushed the arguments back to a still more basic level, where the question is not which authority should prevail but what the genesis and status of any religious authority are. Nor do the positions mentioned in chapters 2 and 3 give much attention to the capacity of the Scriptures to mediate the presence and identity of God. The analogical developmentalist position comes the closest, and its portrait of God is most like the one I have developed. Its focus, however, is more heavily on a philosophical view of the world in process than on the character and identity of God. The other positions skirt a discussion of the capacity of the Scriptures to mediate the presence and identity of God because they assume a more classical understanding of God. To postmodern thought the classical understanding seems far less secure than it once did, since cultural developments have here too pushed us back to more basic issues—where the question concerns not merely the distinctiveness of Christianity over against Deism but the dynamics of belief in any God. None of the modern positions distinguish between the kerygmatic and the confessional, and none develop principles by which to distinguish different levels of authority. Over against the tendencies of the rationalists to pick and choose from the Bible, they try to establish a view that gives uniform authority to the Bible as a whole.

Thus, I have drawn insights from each of the four viable modern positions, though I have rearranged and expanded the ingredients into an approach significantly different from any that furnished the insights. Because the cultural context has changed, the whole thrust of the theory that I am prcposing is different. It addresses different issues and makes quite different appeals.

7

Recontextualizing the Bible

Chapters 4, 5, and 6 have addressed a cluster of questions associated with a contemporary view of the Bible: Why turn to the Bible? What does it have to offer a postmodern society? What can a person reasonably expect to find in the Bible? The questions are important because they relate to expectations, and everyone in the community of faith brings to the Bible one or another set of expectations, which need to be isolated, examined, and evaluated. Are they appropriate to the character of the Bible and its role in the church?

Even where there are only appropriate expectations, however, there are still difficulties. The point of view I have defended in this book says that an authority relationship develops as the Bible is used in the community of faith. But *how* is the Bible to be used? How is it to be interpreted and applied? My answer, in a word, is that the passages of the Bible need to be "recontextualized." The biblical message needs to be spoken anew in such a way as to have the same impact in the contemporary situation that it had in its original setting.[1]

Let us say that a child listens to her mother's advice. When the child encounters a new situation similar to the one that elicited this advice, she must decide whether it still applies. Her decision is a simple form of recontextualizing. The more similar the two situations, the more likely it is that the advice can be transferred without alteration. When the same child moves away from home, she may well confront a setting in which she has to do something quite new in order to remain true to her mother's advice. This too is recontextualizing. Being true to advice does not necessarily mean unthinking imitation or obedience. It means a careful assessment of the intended effect of the original words and the likely effect of the several courses of action possible in the new setting. To recontextualize appropriately is to choose the course of action most in harmony with the original impact of the words.

In order to be used appropriately, the Scriptures, too, must be recontextualized. Even more care must be taken here than by the child away from home, because the temporal, social, cultural, and geographic distance is so much greater.

Historical Distance

For recontextualizing to occur, historical distance must be recognized. The interpreter must acknowledge and appreciate the significant differences of social custom and cultural perspective that separate the time of writing from the present. The differences are not peripheral but affect the shape of the very message. Historical criticism is a disciplined procedure to help us recognize temporal distance. It defamiliarizes texts.[2] Its distancing is important because the Bible does not usually share today's priorities and ways of thinking. Only a very selective and ahistorical reading can make it appear to do so.

Though one should not stop with the initial step of historical distancing, the step can itself be creative. By encountering a set of traditions with which we are linked—so that they cannot be dismissed as totally alien—and yet recognizing the differences, we are made aware of the finitude of our own ways, even those ways we consider most influenced by our Christian faith.[3] Ours are not the only possible patterns of thought and behavior. It takes some imagination, some self-distancing, to enter into the world of the past. Entering the past may in turn stimulate a different sort of imaginative endeavor: that of imagining more just and humane ways to structure our contemporary life.

The imaginative turn to the future occurs within the Bible itself and is an essential element in the reform-oriented vitality of Christianity. In the totalitarian society of Orwell's *1984* all records of the past that portray a reality different from the present are destroyed and rewritten to reflect the current outlook of the party leaders; they are rewritten in order to stifle creative reform. Only if alternatives are perceived to be possible can reform become a genuine option. The interpreter must not ignore or camouflage the distance separating the text from our town times, since the difference can be salutary. Not only does it safeguard the integrity—the overagainstness—of the text but it also stimulates contemporary human beings to consider alternatives to present patterns of thought and action.

The Original Context

For recontextualization to occur, information about the original context of a passage must be available. In what setting were the words first spoken? In what setting and for what reason were they preserved, written down, edited, and canonized?[5] Historical-critical investigation can supply that indispensable information about a text. Though historical criticism is the source of few certainties, because it is in principle always open to new discoveries and new arrangements of what is known, it has shown itself to be relatively public, that is, relatively immune to the influence of prior theological commitments, and in this sense relatively scientific. Exegetes from a variety of denominations and even from

different religions can agree that a particular passage in its original setting "must have meant this" or "could not have meant that." The interpreter needs to have as much information as possible about the historical
setting and literary context of a passage, and historical criticism can
uncover that information.

Only with such information can the original meaning of the text
be ascertained. Were it true that words and sentences always have the
same meaning, irrespective of the setting in which they are used, historical-critical analysis would be a waste of effort. One could move directly
from the text to application without recontextualizing. But meaning is
context-dependent. The same sentence can have an impact in one setting quite different from its impact in another. A prohibition against
alcohol, for example, meant one thing to eighteenth-century Method-
ists who had been uprooted and displaced into factory towns—who
had experienced despair and the attraction of chemical abuse and had
then found in Wesley's "classes" a support group and new meaning for
their lives. But it meant quite another when restated to their middle-
class, twentieth-century descendants living in a small town in a "dry
county" in the rural United States. In its earlier setting, a sermon
encouraging people to avoid alcohol would have seemed "in touch" with
the very real struggle they were experiencing and would have seemed
supportive. In the later setting, the same sermon would likely be out of
touch with people's real struggles; it would seem to apply to someone
else somewhere else and therefore only encourage a self-righteous
moralism. The words would be the same, but because the setting influences what the words communicate, the impact of the words would be
much different.

In order to understand the original meaning of a passage, one
must understand its meaning in context, for which historical-critical study
is an indispensable tool. Though a postmodern theory of biblical
authority cannot be founded on what seemed in modern culture to be
the solid rock of historicity, it also cannot dispense with the discipline
of historical study.

The Contemporary Context

In order for there to be recontextualization, however, information must be gathered not only about the original setting of the text but
also about the setting within which the interpretation is to be received.
The interpreter must understand the contemporary audience. What are
their struggles, their assumptions, their priorities? How will a particular statement strike them? In the deepest sense, no one can predict with

accuracy how someone will respond. There is no substitute for listening for the actual response. But the interpreter needs to know as much as possible about the contemporary setting. The interpreter needs to read the signs of the times and sense what deep existential, moral, and religious issues are troubling contemporary human beings. That means, among other things, studying the character of the times, listening to those most pained by today's society to determine the source and character of their pain (because it probably affects the rest of us as well), paying attention to artists and poets, paying attention to descriptions of our society that come from other cultures (even those antagonistic to our own), and cultivating the capacity for empathy.

It is never easy to discern the signs of the times. Some people are more adept at this than others, but all need the give-and-take of a supportive community in which to explore and assess perceptions. By comparing the partial insights each community member may have, the group as a whole can achieve a deeper insight into contemporary society and what it is like for human beings to live in it. At its best the church is a community engaged in precisely this kind of exploration. In order to fill its role in the exploration, the church cannot be organized in an authoritarian way, with clergy or theologians calling all the shots or with teachings and ethical norms imposed as if they supplied all the necessary answers or needed only to be received and accepted in a nonparticipatory fashion. In order for the community of faith to function as it is here expected to do, it must be a genuine community in which the insights of all contribute to the overall understanding of the present.[6] Especially important are the insights gained by laity from their weekday occupations. Such insights serve as windows onto contemporary society, onto that very society which must be understood in order for recontextualization to occur.

The interpreter needs to understand the people who will receive the biblical message because the impact of the interpretation occurs as it encounters people and interacts with their lives. In order to assess the impact of any set of words, one must understand how the hearers interact with the words and understand the results of the interaction in their lives.

None of this is meant to deny that the insights of the Bible can help us interpret the signs of the times. The movement is reciprocal. As we move back and forth from the historical setting of the Scriptures to our present condition, we begin to discern aspects of the present that previously escaped our attention. That too is an important part of discerning the contemporary context within which contextualization is to occur.

The Correlation of Impact

Recontextualization involved a comparison between the impact of the words of the Bible at the time of their original articulation and the impact of similar or different words today. A correct and setting-relevant interpretation is one for which the impact on a set of hearers today is as similar as possible to the text's impact on its original hearers and readers. When interpretation achieves this, the text has been successfully recontextualized.

Consider an example. From the best information available to us, it seems clear that the first chapter of Genesis was originally written by priests for the benefit of Israelites during the exile. The exiles were attracted by the splendor of Babylon. They wondered whether the gods of Babylon had not defeated the God of Israel and asked themselves what had happened to the promises upon which Israel had been built now that the nation had been destroyed. The priestly author or authors of the first chapter of Genesis wanted to reassure people living amid the chaos of seemingly shattered promises, of a defeated nation, and of a disrupted social and religious life—the temple having been destroyed—that God was still at work bringing order out of chaos. They wanted to reassure the people that the promises of God were rooted in the very nature of creation. Thus the emphasis in the first chapter of Genesis is on the ordering activity of God. The intended impact is to restore hope in God's promises and loyalty to the God of Israel. God brought order out of chaos in the past, and God will bring order out of the chaos being experienced by the readers of this text. Seen in its original setting, Genesis 1 is primarily about the future, not the past.

In order to interpret and apply the message of Genesis 1, it must be recontextualized. In our day that is easily done, because many Christians are experiencing pressures and questions very similar to those of the Israelites during the exile. Chaos seems more evident than order. The promise once associated with the American nation is now dubious. A secular culture devoted to other gods offers tremendous appeal. People wonder, Where will it all come out? What is the use of remaining faithful amid such chaos? An appropriate recontextualizing focuses on the promises of God that continue valid: God is with us. Blessed are the poor. Blessed are the peacemakers. An appropriate recontextualizing generates hope in the continuing work of God in creating a humane and just order out of chaos.

Differences of Setting

Recontextualizing obviously works better for some passages than for others. If the original setting of a passage is very different from the setting addressed by an interpreter, the passage may be difficult to recontextualize in an adequate and discerning way. (Apparently this realization led both Luther and Calvin to avoid any commentary on the Apocalypse.) But the passage is not therefore useless, for it may become very important at another time—as Hanns Lilje, one of Luther's descendants, discovered the Apocalypse to become during the Nazi totalitarianism of World War II Germany.[7] Nor does the passage become nonscriptural or noncanonical, for the canon by its very nature encompasses passages that reflect, and therefore relate to, a wide variety of settings. What is true, though, is that in any setting some passages will have a greater claim on the community than others.

In actual use, then, the Bible does not exercise a uniform degree or kind of authority within the community of faith. At any particular time and place, because authority grows out of use and usefulness, some parts of the Bible will have greater actual authority than others. How should an interpreter proceed when a passage is encountered whose original setting is unlike the circumstances of the interpreter's audience?

First of all, the interpreter must not assume that the difference in settings renders the passage useless for the community in the present. After all, individuals often face problems that are not faced by society as a whole. For example, a person may experience chaos even if order prevails in society as a whole. That person can find something in Genesis 1 that the well-ordered society may not immediately hear. Moreover, people are able to empathize with others whose circumstances are different from their own, so long as the difference is pointed out and recognized. They can benefit from a discussion of the way God has cared for people in other situations, for this can reassure them of the steadfast love of God that would do the same for them if they faced comparable difficulties. It can also reassure them that the presence of God does not depend on the present political, economic, social, and personal order. If this order were to disappear, God would still be here.

Second, when the present setting differs from the historical context of a passage, the interpreter must first of all imagine a contemporary setting similar to the original context of the passage and then draw only those implications which would not violate the kind of impact the text would have in the imagined setting. For example, if an interpreter of Genesis 1 lives in a setting where there is a great deal of order, maybe even tyranny, it will not be possible to move directly from Genesis 1 to the contemporary setting. Rather, the interpreter will first have to imagine contemporary circumstances that are riddled with chaos. Whatever the interpretation given Genesis 1, it must not violate the impact the text would have in the imagined chaotic setting. Thus, to interpret the passage as saying that God is trying to create still more order would be inappropriate, for the passage's impact would then be confining instead of liberating, bad news instead of good news. Its impact would be different from what it was for the Israelites in exile.

At minimum, imagining a situation similar to that of the text can forestall misinterpretations of the passage. The concepts used by the author or authors of Genesis 1 reflect the best science of the day, adapted for the purpose of reassuring the Israelites in exile of God's working to bring order out of chaos. The emphasis in the creation account on order and on the role of the spoken word indicates an outlook that remains the underlying premise of modern science: that nature is knowable and not capricious, in that an experiment done today can be repeated tomorrow with the same results. Consequently, interpretations of Genesis 1 that see it as opposing scientific theories about the beginning of the world are misinterpretations. If its authors were able to use the best science of their day, the interpreter should be able to draw upon the best science of our day, without allowing scientific theories to dictate the meaning of the passage. Even if the original and contemporary contexts are so different that we cannot decide exactly what the author or authors would say in the contemporary setting, we can at least rule out some possibilities. By imagining a situation in which priests might be living in exile today, we can at least determine that an antiscience interpretation of Genesis 1 is misconceived. Such an interpretation would not merely go beyond but would go against the text's impact in its original setting.

When a passage written in one setting is interpreted in an extremely different setting, the application is thus less direct than when the settings are similar. An extra step is involved: that of imagining a contemporary context like the original. The extra step must be carried out carefully, but when it is, it enhances the fidelity and significance of the contemporary interpretation.

The Integrity of the Biblical Message

What then safeguards the integrity of the biblical message? What prevents the community from selecting those texts that reinforce its own attitudes and priorities and from dismissing those which challenge or confront the status quo?

The emphasis on assessing contextual similarity can discipline—and ought to discipline—the use of the Bible so as to prevent a co-opting of it. It can prevent importance from being ascribed to only those passages that reinforce rather than confront one's current biases.

For example, the Puritans who came to Massachusetts interpreted the New World as the promised land. They saw a similarity between their setting and that of the Israelites during the time of the exodus and the conquest. Both the Puritans and the Israelites had been rescued by God from a land of oppression, both had crossed a sea in safety, both had entered a new and perilous promised land. Their task was to make of their new home a "light to the nations," a beacon of hope. The Puritans' recontextualization was plausible; it gave to a band of immigrants, camped precariously on the edge of an unfamiliar continent, a bold sense of mission and purpose, an incentive to create a humane, just, and free society. At its best it challenged their provincial insularity and expanded their vision. Except to the Native Americans—and this came, tragically, to be a very significant exception—it did no one any harm.

The Puritans' interpretation is frequently repeated today, as if it still applies to the United States. But does it? A comparison of settings indicates that it does not. The Puritans were powerless; the contemporary United States possesses enormous power and influence. The Puritans saw themselves beginning anew; a two-hundred-year-old nation is not beginning anew. The Puritans shared a single religious outlook; contemporary citizens do not. Though not exactly equal, the Puritans were all of poor to middling means; enormous inequities now characterize our society, making it in this regard more like the one the Puritans left behind. If the Puritans were to describe the contemporary United States, might they not find it more like the Egypt of the pharaohs than the Israel of the exodus? The original and contemporary settings are now too dissimilar to make the interpretation begun by the Puritans a plausible recontextualizing of the biblical text.

Anyone wishing to interpret the Bible to contemporary Americans must seek a paradigm from another set of passages whose context is more similar to our own. Would our setting not, for example, be more like that of later Judah, blithely finding security in earlier announcements (such as Nathan's promises to David regarding the future of his descendants on the throne) while ignoring the injustices and inequities in its midst, or blithely assuming that God so much wants it to endure that any means to this end, no matter how destructive, are justified? The setting of later Judah is far less appealing to contemporary Americans looking for a historical prototype of their own context than the accounts of the exodus and the conquest. But it is also probably a more accurate parallel, capable of producing interpretations which are more faithful to the text.

The Bible says quite different things depending on which passages are appropriate to one's context. For the integrity of the text to be

136

safeguarded, the choice needs to be disciplined by a careful comparison of settings. Only that can prevent passages from being applied selectively or having their meaning distorted by inherited patterns.

Diversity as an Asset

Recontextualizing provides a mode of interpretation in which scriptural diversity becomes an asset rather than an embarrassing liability. This happens in several ways. First, recognizing scriptural diversity acknowledges the occasional character of almost all the documents found in the Bible. Each document is addressed to a specific people living at a particular time and in a particular place. Each attempts to achieve fairly clear and specific purposes. A message that was highly specific to its original setting can, however, be applied and embodied concretely in another. Strangely enough, occasional writing is more transferable than is abstract writing. In 1 Corinthians, for example, Paul wrestles with very specific problems, but his message is more easily recontextualized than is some of the abstract philosophy written by his contemporaries.

Second, recognizing scriptural diversity helps to make the Scriptures a resource for communities living in widely divergent temporal, geographical, and cultural circumstances. For every age, a word can be found somewhere within the scope of the Bible. Correctly interpreted, the Bible may not say exactly the same things to a tribe uninfluenced by Western society that it does to an American congregation; the same text may "mean" different things. But that is not a problem; it is an asset, because it enables the claim of God that comes through the text to be accessible to both. The interpretations worked out in an American congregation should not be imposed on fellow Christians in other cultures without benefit of a careful reinterpretation.

Third, recognizing scriptural diversity helps lift the sights of the reader beyond the propositions, ideas, and recommendations being expressed, to the God whose presence is informing all the diverse statements. From the diversity one can sense that something greater must be at stake. By exploring that dimension, the reader comes to glimpse the presence of God.

Finally, recognizing the diversity within the Bible encourages the reader to acknowledge the diversity that characterizes an authentic community. The unity of a community is not to be discovered in uniformity. A variety of emphases, abilities, and perspectives are needed, even within a single congregation. The catholicity of the Scriptures permits an ecumenical vision of the inclusiveness of the whole Christian

137

church. The unity of the Bible is to be sought not within the Bible but in that to which the various parts of the Bible point: God. Likewise, the unity of the church is to be found not within the church but in the God who has called the church into being. Given this understanding of the unity of Scripture, the diversity exhibited there is not a liability but an asset. It can be recognized, analyzed, and explored—perhaps even celebrated—with profit.

The Priority of Kerygma and Story

Recontextualization works with two additional priorities, both of which grow out of this book's earlier discussions of scriptural authority. First, the kerygmatic has priority over the confessional. If the setting of a kerygmatic message is similar enough to the contemporary context for its kerygmatic content to be recontextualized successfully, then an appropriate confessional response can be inferred. To seek to recontextualize a confessional response found in the Scriptures without regard to the kerygmatic message upon which it is based, however, causes harm. The movement is from the kerygmatic to the confessional. The kerygmatic cannot be inferred from the confessional without distortions resulting.

It is, for example, inappropriate to attempt to recontextualize the confessional dimension of the Bible by extracting an ethical injunction from one of Paul's letters and trying to apply it to contemporary society without regard to the kerygmatic message from which Paul infers his advice. Inappropriate extrapolation occurs when Paul's references to homosexuality are interpreted to mean that homosexuals should be excluded from the church, for the kerygmatic point Paul is making is that God's mercy extends beyond every expected limit. An ethics of exclusion cannot be inferred from Paul's kerygma, because his kerygma moves in the opposite direction. In order to avoid error, the interpreter must recontextualize the kerygmatic before ascertaining whether and how the confessional response embodied in the text may also be recontextualized today.

Second, in a postmodern society, storytelling takes priority over doctrinal and ethical specification. The Bible is the story of God's interaction with God's people told in such a way as to reveal the identity and character of God and, correlatively, to form and inform the identity of the community of faith. Story is the right medium to convey a sense of another's identity. If I, for example, described my wife to you, I could give you all sorts of information about her (height, weight, eye color, college grade-point average, place of birth, and so on), and I could give you abstract descriptions (she is intelligent, ethical, and industrious). But not until I began to tell you stories about how she reacts in this or that setting will her unique identity begin to be communicated. The best way to discern God's character and identity is through narratives about how God has reacted and interacted with people.

Story plays a role in building any human identity. Only if I know my life has a story do I know who I am, and only if I see my life as part of a larger epic does the story of my life begin to take on meaning. Where the overarching story is already known, it may not need to be retold, but when the Christian story is not already built into the symbols and values of the culture—as it is not in postmodern culture—storytelling is an indispensable medium for communicating the Christian message.

In our setting it is thus inappropriate to derive doctrinal or ethical lessons from biblical stories until the full impact of their story character has been communicated, received, and acknowledged.[8] Even then, however, doctrinal lessons need to be tested to see whether they reflect clearly and accurately the identity of God, and ethical lessons need to be tested to see whether they embody clearly and effectively the appropriate, correlative identity of the Christian community. None of this implies that doctrines or ethical guidelines are unimportant. Doctrines, at their best, are transparent to God in much the same way that the Scriptures themselves are transparent to God. They are, moreover, forged by the church in much the same way that the biblical documents were composed, and they must be recontextualized in order to be understood. The difference is merely that doctrines have meaning only when the underlying story is known, whereas the Scriptures are a direct witness to that story. In short, doctrines are recontextualizations of Scripture, the Scriptures are not recontextualizations of doctrine.

Because doctrines point back to the message of the Scriptures and are dependent upon their witness and their insights, the importance of the biblical story in a postmodern setting should not be overlooked. Doctrines are valuable but cannot substitute for the story itself.

The Imagination

Recontextualization involves the imagination. Despite the discipline imposed by the necessity of comparing settings, each new interpretation should retell the story in an imaginative way—not, that is, in fanciful flights from reality but by means of fresh images and metaphors. The use of biblical language is important but by itself is no guarantee that the message is being adequately recontextualized. Biblical language may or may not convey to the contemporary hearers what

139

it did to the original hearers. If it does not, then fresh, arresting words have to be fashioned that make an impact similar to the original. For that, creativity and imagination are needed, however much they also need to be disciplined.

Imagination is necessary also because the interpreter must enter empathically into the world of his or her hearers and envisage the likely impact of the proposed interpretation. Empathic efforts to foresee an interpretation's impact involve imagination, since they must be made in advance. Even if they follow an initial interpretation that has produced an unintended and inappropriate impact, they still occur in advance of the next interpretation attempted.

No Guarantee

One caution is in order. No theory of biblical authority and no set of procedures can guarantee that correct and setting-relevant interpretations will be produced, nor can they guarantee unanimity among interpreters or among those who listen to the same interpretation. There are several reasons for this.

Recontextualization involves a disciplined imagination. It is very difficult to hold discipline and imagination together here, since quite different approaches and activities are involved in historical analysis and in an imaginative reconstruction of the biblical story. The context for interpretation remains the community of faith, and only the give-and-take of a variety of perspectives and capabilities can help keep the process one that is simultaneously under the discipline of careful historical study and in movement toward imaginative proclamation, interpretation, and application.

Again, recontextualization often involves a challenge to the status quo of the interpreter as well as of the hearer. Recontextualization requires growth and change; it requires dealing with hitherto unrecognized or unacknowledged challenges and possibilities. It therefore demands a level of spiritual maturity not realized fully in any single individual nor uniformly in any group of individuals. Change is never popular and never self-evidently good. A host of psychological—to say nothing of economic, intellectual, and social—interests are lodged against any significant existential reorientation. Recontextualization also challenges the societal and cultural status quo. Though aspects of the familiar may be affirmed, no society is so uniformly Christian as to harmonize totally with the kingdom of God. None escapes the arresting challenge of the biblical message.

Interpretation easily vacillates between a disengaged, unempathic rejection of the present and an uncritical endorsement of contemporary values. A close examination of conservative and critical interpreters will quickly reveal that neither group is exempt from excess. And when they fall victim to it, they differ merely in what features of the present they uncritically endorse or unempathically reject.

Recontextualization also challenges the religious status quo. It is far easier to repeat interpretations that were marvelously insightful in the past than to be challenged by those having a great—and perhaps even a perplexing—claim on us in the present. Interpreters easily vacillate between preserving the insights of earlier interpreters and overlooking or dismissing their contributions to a deeper understanding of the text. Interpreters should not ignore the history of interpretation, because the interaction of text and community helps to reveal the rich depth of the text and its message. But neither should the profundity of the past seduce interpreters into neglecting the far riskier task of recontextualization.

The community of faith engenders the support necessary for risking a new interpretation and supplies the wisdom to keep it focused. In the community of faith new interpretations are subjected to the scrutiny of others who have been in the presence of God. There too they can be refined through study and debate. Throughout the process the Spirit continues present and active.

Still another reason that unanimity is not guaranteed is that interpretation is in the end more an art than a science. Theories and procedures can assist in interpretation, the public information provided by historical criticism can enrich it, but it remains a skill to be cultivated and refined, a skill requiring empathy, imagination, risk taking, and wisdom.

There is nothing new about the controversies that interpretation engenders. The community of faith has throughout its history included persons who claimed to have a message directly from God and therefore of the utmost urgency and highest authority. The community of faith has had to adjudicate the sometimes rival claims, each uttered in the name of the Lord. Jeremiah faced two hundred prophets, all of whom claimed to speak the "word of the Lord" and all of whom announced a message quite the opposite of his own. Ultimately the community of faith decided that Jeremiah's minority voice was authentic and dismissed the other two hundred as false prophets. To side with Jeremiah was risky. Discerning the word of God in his message was more an art than a science.

In the late second century C.E., those trying to make decisions about the New Testament canon were faced with many documents claiming to be inspired. Under pressure from Gnosticism and Montanism, the community had to decide which of the many documents were apostolic in content. Eventually only one book that claimed to be an inspired document was accepted into the New Testament: the Apocalypse of John. It was judged to be apostolic in a way that other now noncanonical works were not. The community needed to make this decision. It had to adjudicate conflicting claims. Some were rejected; others were accepted.

It is thus not surprising that no guidelines can ever guarantee that interpretations of the Bible will be self-evident or without dispute or controversy. Even those who agree on a single theory of biblical authority do not all share the same interpretation of every passage. In fact, one can expect that interpretations relevant to the interpreter's setting will be controversial, because they challenge members of the church to change and to grow. Correct and setting-relevant interpretations rely on the inspiration of the Spirit and the insight and wisdom of the community of faith, which interact in such a way that the Spirit may work through the full range of diversity found in the community and that unanticipated insights into God's current activity may be discovered.

Breaking Open

An appropriate recontextualizing of the Scriptures tells a story in such a way as to break the present open to transcendence. It breaks open the present by opening it to the insights of the past. It breaks it open by introducing a vision of the future. And it breaks it open by pointing beyond itself to the identity of God and the correlative identity of the community.

The model for recontextualizing is Jesus' own storytelling. The story of the Good Samaritan is told in answer to the question, Who is my neighbor? Jesus, however, breaks the question open by asking, "Which of these three... proved neighbor to the man who fell among the robbers?" (Luke 10:29-37). On another occasion he accepts the messianic designation offered by Peter's confession but then breaks it open by pointing to his own suffering (Mark 8:27-31).

Not only should the storytelling of the community of faith provide an overarching story within which the contemporary human being can find a meaningful role but it should break open that story to make visible the presence and existential claims of the transcendent God in the life of each hearer. Unless it does so it will merely instill a cosmology or ideology; it will not perform its primary task of pointing beyond itself to God and God's identity. The original revelation made existential claims on people as it called the community of faith into being and as it sustained the community through renewed calls. A recontextualizing of the Scriptures is incomplete without the same calls being heard today. Whatever historical distance separates the contemporary church from the Bible, in the reissuance of the original call it encounters the same God. The distance is bridged not by the interpreter but by God and the inspiring presence of the Spirit. The Bible retains its authority because it continues to mediate to the community of faith God's call and presence. Within the community the Bible *becomes* the Word of God and a means of grace. In the ongoing task of mediating God's call, inspiration is at work. Since no procedure can guarantee the truth of an interpretation—even the interpretation of an inspired text—the inspiring presence of the Spirit is indispensable. Either the Spirit is at work in the contemporary community as it interprets the Scriptures or nothing can redeem the Scriptures' authority.

Embodiment

The procedures involved in recontextualizing the Scriptures focus, inform, enliven, and discipline the process of interpretation. Though the Scriptures should be understood and applied carefully, the ultimate goal of interpretation is not only to understand. Embodiment is the ultimate goal. The Scriptures mediate the presence of God, an arresting, transforming, identity-forming, and relationship-forming presence. An encounter with the presence of God calls for an existential response to be embodied in a renewed life that lives the shalom of God's kingdom.

Ezekiel, during his call to become a prophet, was handed a written scroll and commanded to eat it. "Son of man, eat what is offered to you; eat this scroll, and go, speak to the house of Israel" (Ezek. 3:1). The episode provides a vivid image of how the Scriptures are to be internalized, influencing every fiber of a person's being and identity. The goal of recontextualizing is that God's Word be embodied in the lives, words, and actions of contemporary human beings.

EPILOGUE

"Take it and read it. Take it and read it." Those words, spoken by a child, were heard by Saint Augustine while he, deeply troubled, sat next to a Bible in a garden.[1] Augustine picked up the Bible and read, and the verse he read spoke to his perplexities and ended his hesitation about the Christian faith. A similar voice says to the community of faith today, "Take it and read it." The Bible speaks only when it is used.

The Bible's authority is honored most not when lofty claims are made in its behalf but when it is used in the community of faith and embodied in the daily lives of the community's members. From such use comes its authority. The most fitting conclusion to this book is therefore an invitation to participate in recontextualizing the Bible. You are invited to gather with others to study and interpret the Bible, to try on the principles I have enunciated, to test them, and to see whether they enable the arresting claim of biblical texts to come through.

I have written this volume, not to put forward a theory to carry in one's mind, but to identify some procedures that illumine the Bible's claim on our own priorities. These efforts have value if they lead to greater use of the Bible and help break open its message, for that message of God's caring presence is what inspires and nourishes lives faithful to God's call.

NOTES

Introduction

1. Cf. John Ruemann, *Righteousness in the New Testament: Justification in Lutheran-Catholic Dialogue* (Philadelphia: Fortress Press, 1983).
2. Brevard S. Childs, *Introduction to the Old Testament as Scripture* (Philadelphia: Fortress Press, 1979), 16. Emphasis mine.
3. Ibid., 41.
4. Ibid., 75.
5. Walter Wink, *The Bible in Human Transformation: Toward a New Paradigm for Biblical Study* (Philadelphia: Fortress Press, 1973), 1.
6. Ibid., 2-15.
7. Paul Ricoeur, *The Symbolism of Evil* (New York: Harper & Row, 1967), 352. Ricoeur argues that comparison and criticism introduce a neutralized distance, which disrupts the original immediacy of belief. The "second immediacy" is a third stage, within which the existential truth of a symbol or story is reaffirmed.
8. I believe there is such a thing as a Christian humanism, which overlaps at some points with non-Christian humanism, thus making cooperation possible. I acknowledge that some, particularly some conservative, Christians now equate humanism with "godless secularism" and therefore consider it anathema, but I do not accept that equation. Secularism is the belief that human life is full and complete without reference to God or any transcendent realities. Humanism is an ethical stance committed to the preservation of human dignity and societal justice, with or without reference to God. I prefer to refer to secularism as secularism and reserve the term *humanism* for more constructive purposes. The consequences for social ethics and public policy are very significant.

1. Authority as Problematic in the Modern Era

1. From team-teaching a freshman humanities course on the "perils and potentials of twentieth-century life," I have learned that professors of art, literature, philosophy, and history can agree on a portrait of modern culture much like the one described in this chapter.
2. This difference came about in part because the Middle Ages and modern culture were focusing on different problems: the Middle Ages were striving to build a cohesive society, whereas modern culture—which could assume a cohesive society—focused its efforts on technological innovation. Each generalized into other areas of life an approach that was fruitful in the area of its primary concern.
3. The most famous example of this approach is the set of lectures on the "essence of Christianity" given at the University of Berlin by Adolf von

147

Harnack in 1899-1900 and published in English under the title *What Is Christianity?* (Philadelphia: Fortress Press, 1986).

4. A position taken since the 1880s by numerous fundamentalists in the United States and, more recently, in a somewhat different way, by the creationists.

5. Genesis 1 proclaims that the sun, moon, stars, animals, fish, birds—indeed, natural things of any sort—are not to be worshiped and accorded the respect of sacred objects but are to be seen as creatures of the one and only God. They are given to human beings, who are to care for and use them. Moreover, God is portrayed as ordering the created world; what has been ordered can be analyzed and understood.

6. This general pattern of thinking is represented by Gabriel Biel. See Heiko Oberman, *The Harvest of Medieval Theology: Gabriel Biel and Late Medieval Nominalism* (Cambridge: Harvard Univ. Press, 1963), 57-111, 390-98.

7. See Bruce Vawter, *Biblical Inspiration* (Philadelphia: Westminster Press, 1972), 78-79.

8. The criterion was apostolicity. See Hans von Campenhausen, *The Formation of the Christian Bible* (Philadelphia: Fortress Press, 1972), 205, 217, 253-61, 315-21.

9. It is interesting to note that inspiration became theologically significant in the ancient church only when—as in the case of Origen—an allegorical interpretation of the text needed justification. Only if the text was inspired by God could one be confident that it held hidden spiritual meanings. The same thinking was at work in the post-Reformation era: e.g., only if the text was inspired could passages from the Old Testament be used as evidence for the doctrine of the Trinity.

10. Vawter, *Biblical Inspiration*, 47; see also 154-155.

11. Unfortunately, there is no single good study to refer the reader to for an understanding of the post-Reformation period. The portrait presented here is the author's own, pieced together from various sources, many of which treat the subject only indirectly. In any case, the sources are too numerous to enumerate here. Some help can be gleaned from Heinrich Schmid's *The Doctrinal Theology of the Evangelical Lutheran Church* (Minneapolis: Augsburg Pub. House, 1961); Robert P. Scharlemann's *Thomas Aquinas and John Gerhard* (New Haven: Yale Univ. Press, 1964); and Robert D. Preus's *The Theology of Post-Reformation Lutheranism*, 2 vols. (St. Louis: Concordia Pub. House, 1970-72).

12. See Ernest Sandeen, who writes, with regard to the American scene, "Most twentieth-century Fundamentalists and many twentieth-century historians have mistakenly assumed that Protestantism possessed a strong, fully integrated theology of biblical authority which was attacked by advocates of the higher criticism. As we shall see, no such theology existed before 1850. What did exist was a great deal of popular reverence for the Bible, the eighteenth-century literature defending the authenticity of the Scriptures and providing 'evidences' of their supernatural origin—all of which was beside the point—and an apologetic stance which had con-

Notes

ditioned defenders of the faith to respond to any challenge to the Bible with the cry 'heresy.' A systematic theology of biblical authority which defended the common evangelical faith in the infallibility of the Bible had to be created in the midst of the nineteenth-century controversy" (*The Roots of Fundamentalism: British and American Millenarianism, 1800-1930* [Grand Rapids: Baker Book House, 1978], 106).

13. Martin Marty makes a similar point when, regarding the Protestant reactionaries at the turn of the century, he writes, "They chose to literalize some of the very biblical language that earlier orthodoxy had treated as allegory, metaphor, or as too obscure for precise application to the world of the day's newspapers. To classify these inventions as conservative is imprecise, since many of them were fresh statements, not retentions" (*Modern American Religion*, vol. 1, *The Irony of It All, 1893-1919* [Chicago: Univ. of Chicago Press, 1986], 219. *Countermodern* is a term I borrow from Marty's volume.

14. See Voltaire's "Sermon of the Fifty" as one example of such polemics. It can be found in *Deism: An Anthology*, ed. Peter Gay (Princeton: D. Van Nostrand, 1968), 143-58.

15. See, e.g., Karl Marx's introduction to his "Contribution to the Critique of Hegel's Philosophy of Right," in *Karl Marx and Friedrich Engels on Religion* (New York: Schocken Books, 1964), 41-58.

16. Although I have written these comments with nineteenth-century Europe in mind, they can be applied to recent debates in the United States regarding the Moral Majority and others who appeal to the Bible in support of a reactionary or conservative political program.

17. The *Proslogium* can be found in *St. Anselm: Basic Writings*, trans. S. N. Deane (La Salle, Ill.: Open Court, 1962), 1-34.

18. One discussion of Anselm's argument that is without reference to its original setting is in Wallace I. Matson's *The Existence of God* (Ithaca, N.Y.: Cornell Univ. Press, 1965), 43-55. Matson is concerned with the internal logic of the argument and treats the argument in the abstract.

19. Robert Preus, *Theology of Post-Reformation Lutheranism*, 1:181-82.

2. Responses within a Static World View

1. David Kelsey, *The Uses of Scripture in Recent Theology* (Philadelphia: Fortress Press, 1975), 166.

2. The portrait I sketch here is a composite, but among the names one could associate with rationalism are John Toland (*Christianity Not Mysterious*, 1696), Matthew Tindal (*Christianity as Old as Creation*, 1730), Thomas Paine (*The Age of Reason*, 1795), Ernest Renan, Voltaire (e.g., *"Sermon of the Fifty"*) Reimarus (whose Fragments were published by Lessing in the 1770s), and to a certain degree, David Friedrich Strauss (*Life of Jesus*, 1835). Strauss, however, is a transitional figure whose thought contains elements of a more developmentalist outlook, such as one finds in dynamic humanism. For a brief summary of Toland's thought and Paine's theology, see James C. Livingston, *Modern Christian Thought: From the Enlightenment to*

Vatican II (New York: Macmillan Co., 1971), 20-24. For Voltaire's "Sermon of the Fifty," see *Deism: An Anthology,* ed. Peter Gay (Princeton: D. Van Nostrand, 1968), 143-58. For Reimarus, see *Reimarus: Fragments,* ed. Charles Talbert (Philadelphia: Fortress Press, 1970). See also David Friedrich Strauss, *The Life of Jesus Critically Examined* (Philadelphia: Fortress Press, 1972).

3. A similar point is made by David Nineham in *The Use and Abuse of the Bible: A Study of the Bible in an Age of Rapid Social Change* (New York: Barnes & Noble, 1976), 32-33.

4. The issue surfaces in the writings of Immanuel Kant. For him the existence of freedom is problematic for theoretical reason but is the undergirding assumption of practical (moral) reason. For theoretical reason's conclusions about freedom, see the section of Kant's *Critique of Pure Reason* entitled "The Antinomy of Pure Reason," and for practical reason's, his *Critique of Practical Reason,* as well as his *Fundamental Principles of the Metaphysics of Morals* and *Religion within the Limits of Reason Alone.*

5. The position I describe here was held by the Deists. For a convenient collection of Deist writings, see *Deism,* ed. Gay.

6. A reconstruction of the first compilation, entitled "The Philosophy of Jesus," and a reproduction of the second, entitled "The Life and Morals of Jesus," can be found in *Jefferson's Extracts from the Gospels,* ed. Dickinson W. Adams (Princeton: Princeton Univ. Press, 1983).

7. Thomas Jefferson, letter to William Short, August: 4, 1820, printed in the appendix to *Jefferson's Extracts,* ed. Adams, 396.

8. Ibid.

9. See, e.g., Benjamin Warfield: "We cannot modify the doctrine of plenary inspiration in any of its essential elements without undermining our confidence in the authority of the apostles as teachers of doctrine. . . . Historically, it is attested by the driftage of every school of thought which has sought to find a ground of faith in any lower than the Church's doctrine of a plenarily inspired Bible. The authority which cannot assure of a hard fact is soon not trusted for a hard doctrine. Sooner or later, in greater or less degree, the authority of the Bible in doctrine and life is replaced by or subordinated to that of reason, or of the feelings, or of the 'Christian consciousness' " (*The Works of Benjamin B. Warfield* [Grand Rapids: Baker Book House, 1927] 1:181. Cf. J. Gresham Machen: "Either accept the narratives as they stand, including their supernatural content; or else, without seeking a historical basis in detail, regard them as myths" (*The Virgin Birth of Christ* [New York: Harper & Bros., 1930], 216-17.

10. This was essentially the argument adopted by David Friedrich Strauss in his (in)famous study of the Gospels in 1835 entitled *The Life of Jesus.* Strauss did in fact locate some information he considered to be historically reliable, but his detailed comparisons of Gospel accounts created the impression that the Gospels as a whole were historically unreliable. Strauss was not strictly a rationalist; his interpretation of Christianity moves in the direction of dynamic humanism, to be considered in chap. 3.

11. This paragraph is based on my personal conversations with opponents of historical criticism, who assert that all historical critics allow their reason to judge what is and is not acceptable and that every historical critic is essentially a rationalist. One published document that seems to reflect this view is "A Statement of Scriptural and Confessional Principles," published in the 1970s with a preface by J. A. O. Preus, then president of the Lutheran Church—Missouri Synod. The views specifically rejected in section I of article 4, "Historical Methods of Biblical Interpretation," are those of the rationalists.

12. Such is essentially the argument pioneered by Ferdinand Christian Baur in response to his former pupil David Friedrich Strauss. This position Baur worked out during the fifteen years following the publication of Strauss's *Life of Jesus* in 1835. See Peter C. Hodgson, *The Formation of Historical Theology: A Study of Ferdinand Christian Baur* (New York: Harper & Row, 1966), 78-81; and Ferdinand Christian Baur, *Kritische Untersuchungen über die kanonischen Evangelien: ihr Verhältniss zu einander, ihren Charakter und Ursprung* (Tübingen: Verlag and Druck von Ludw. Fr. Fues, 1847).

13. This portrait too is a composite, but some names to associate with supernaturalism are Ernst W. Hengstenberg (professor of Old Testament at the University of Berlin, 1826-69), Benjamin B. Warfield (professor of theology at Princeton Theological Seminary from 1877 to 1921), Pope Pius X (in his 1907 encyclical, *Pascendi Dominici Gregis,* in which he condemned "modernism" and instituted stringent measures to exclude it from the Roman Catholic church), and J. A. O. Preus (past president of the Lutheran Church—Missouri Synod).

14. *Works of Benjamin B. Warfield* 1:210.

15. Machen, *Virgin Birth,* 217-18. Emphasis mine.

16. Ibid., 385-86.

17. An example of this procedure can be found in James Gray's "The Inspiration of the Bible—Definition, Extent, and Proof," in *The Fundamentals,* by R. A. Torrey et al. (Grand Rapids: Baker Book House, 1917), 2:35-36.

18. William Caven, "The Testimony of Christ to the Old Testament," in *The Fundamentals* 1:217.

19. M. G. Kyle, "The Recent Testimony of Archaeology to the Scriptures," in *The Fundamentals* 1:330.

20. George Frederick Wright, "The Testimony of the Monuments to the Truth of the Scriptures," in *The Fundamentals* 1:303.

21. John H. Gerstner, "A Protestant View of Biblical Authority," in *Scripture in the Jewish and Christian Traditions,* ed. Frederick Greenspahn (Nashville: Abingdon Press, 1982), 57-58.

22. J. A. O. Preus, "A Statement of Scriptural and Confessional Principles," 4A.

23. Ibid., 4F. Emphasis mine.

24. Note that this argument affects questions of dating and authorship. The supernaturalists do not accept the principle that a document must have been written after the last event to which it refers. Because of the unique

ability of biblical authors to foresee accurately, Moses could have written the Pentateuch and foreseen his own death.

25. Those who hold this position would be reluctant to call it the Reed Sea, because that would seem to diminish the extraordinary character of the miracle involved. It would be a compromise that, once taken, would lead one down the slippery slope to naturalism or immanentalism.

26. Evangelicalism can best be associated with a tradition running from John Wesley through revivalism to contemporary "evangelical" Protestantism, Pentecostalism, and neo-Pentecostalism. Though Wesley himself found Scripture and experience to be mutually confirming and thus did not formulate his teachings in the way I have described here, evangelicalism developed within the tradition he inspired. In his own lifetime, Wesley encountered the early stirrings of modern culture and eighteenth-century English rationalism. He regarded the evidence for Christianity to be both external and internal, but he lived at a time when the external proofs were beginning to be controverted, and so he gave relatively greater emphasis than had his predecessors to the internal. He found assurance and joy in the experience of having his heart "strangely warmed," and his evangelicalist descendants sought to encourage the inner experience of the holy Spirit as the basis for religious conviction. A tradition developed, largely popular and unsophisticated, of appealing to a miraculous "awakening" as support for the truth of the Scriptures in particular and the Christian message in general. Outside the Anglo-Saxon world, neopietism provides another example of evangelicalism. Pietism, as distinguished from neopietism, was premodern; it assumed the authority of the Bible and the teachings of orthodoxy and emphasized ways to interiorize and apply those teachings. Neopietism was a modern movement and needed to buttress the authority of the Bible by appeals to inner experience. Claude Welch reports, for example, that for J. C. K. von Hofmann (1810-77), "the 'basis' of Christianity is not actually the 'history of Christ and his apostles'; Christianity rests first of all on 'the present Christ,' who points back to the historical Christ as the presupposition of his presence. . . . Neither in the Bible nor in dogma is certainty available, since both have to be historically investigated, but only in immediate experience" (*Protestant Thought in the Nineteenth Century* [New Haven: Yale Univ. Press, 1972], 1:223-24).

3. Responses within a Dynamic World View

1. Though he would not agree with everything that I impute to ecclesial developmentalism, the father of this approach is Friedrich Schleiermacher (professor of theology at the University of Berlin, 1810-34). Other names associated with it are Albrecht Ritschl (professor of systematic theology at Göttingen, 1864-89) and to a lesser degree Alfred Loisy (French Roman Catholic biblical scholar) as he expressed himself prior to 1904. Loisy's thought includes elements of analogical developmentalism as well. To a considerably lesser degree, Rudolf Bultmann (professor of New Tes-

tament at Marburg, 1921-51) can also be associated with ecclesial developmentalism.

2. Pius X used the latter term in his 1907 encyclical, *Pascendi Dominici Gregis.* The text of *Pascendi Dominici Gregis,* trans. George Tyrrell, can be found in *The Programme of Modernism* (New York: G. P. Putnam's Sons, 1908), 149-245.

3. This was a point of special interest to Albrecht Ritschl, who employed the distinction between *Geist* and *Natur* as a basic category in his theology. See my "Metaphysics and Theology in Albrecht Ritschl," in *Papers of the Nineteenth Century Theology Working Group,* vol. 9 (Berkeley, Calif.: Graduate Theological Union, 1983), 106-17.

4. Three of these predicates—poetic, rhetorical, and didactic—are used by Friedrich Schleiermacher to describe religious language. See his *The Christian Faith* (Edinburgh: T. & T. Clark, 1928), 78.

5. Associated—loosely, I admit—with this view are Georg Wilhelm Friedrich Hegel (professor of philosophy at the University of Berlin, 1818-31), Ferdinand Christian Baur (professor of theology at the University of Tübingen, 1826-60; Baur shares some features of ecclesial developmentalism), and some contemporary process theologians who have been influenced by Alfred North Whitehead and Charles Hartshorne. Many process theologians, however, are endeavoring to articulate a contemporary view that addresses postmodern rather than modern culture. In this way, their thought often reaches beyond analogical developmentalism. For Whitehead's reflections on some of these matters, see his *Religion in the Making* (New York: Macmillan Co., 1926), esp. "Religion and Dogma," 47-80.

6. Georg Wilhelm Friedrich Hegel, *Lectures on the Philosophy of Religion* (Berkeley and Los Angeles: Univ. of California Press, 1984), 1:309.

7. David Griffin, "Relativism, Divine Causation, and Biblical Theology," *Encounter* 36 (1975): 350-51.

8. Ibid., 357. Emphasis omitted.

9. Cf. William Beardslee, who writes, "With God as part of a processively ordered universe, it is possible to make sense of both stability and the emergence of novelty. This way the linear-historical sense of time in the Biblical tradition can be brought into relation with the world of nature, which participates in the same processive order, instead of making history essentially different from nature" (*A House of Hope: A Study in Process and Biblical Thought* [Philadelphia: Westminster Press, 1972], 91).

10. Ibid., 89.

11. Cf. Whitehead, who writes regarding Christianity, "It is the genius of the religion to point at the facts and ask for their systematic interpretation. In the Sermon on the Mount, in the Parables, and in their accounts of Christ, the Gospels exhibit a tremendous fact. The doctrine may, or may not, lie on the surface. But what is primary is the religious fact" (*Religion in the Making,* 51). The term *fact* seems here to mean a "true apprehension of reality."

12. Cf. Jan Van der Veken, who writes, "And yet, the mighty deeds of God are more than just past history: they receive an illuminating (elucidatory) power for all occasions of experience. At this state [for Whitehead] 'religion claims that its concepts, though derived primarily from special experiences, are yet of universal validity, to be applied by faith to the ordering of all experience' " ("Can the True God Be the God of One Book?" in *Religious Experience and Process Theology: The Pastoral Implications of a Major Modern Movement* [New York: Paulist Press, 1976], 269). Van der Veken's quotation is from Whitehead's *Religion in the Making*, 31.

13. Associated with dynamic humanism are Ludwig Feuerbach, Edward Bellamy, the early Karl Marx, and most contemporary humanists.

14. This is a position espoused by Ludwig Feuerbach in *Lectures on the Essence of Religion* (New York: Harper & Row, 1967) and in other writings.

4. The Bible in Postmodern Culture

1. Richard Rubenstein, *The Cunning of History: Mass Death and the American Future* (New York: Harper & Row, 1975), 6-12.

2. Ibid., 12.

3. William Butler Yeats, "The Second Coming," in *The Collected Poems of W. B. Yeats* (New York: Macmillan Co., 1933), 215. The entire verse from which this line is taken reads,

> Turning and turning in the widening gyre
> The falcon cannot hear the falconer;
> Things fall apart; the centre cannot hold;
> Mere anarchy is loosed upon the world,
> The blood-dimmed tide is loosed, and everywhere
> The ceremony of innocence is drowned;
> The best lack all conviction, while the worst
> Are full of passionate intensity.

The poem is from the 1920s.

4. Jaroslav Pelikan made this observation during a lecture, "Lex Orandi, Lex Credendi," delivered May 6, 1979, at Drew University, Madison, New Jersey. He addressed a joint plenary session of the Eastern Metropolitan Region of the American Academy of Religion, the Metropolitan and Eastern Pennsylvania Regions of the College Theology Society, and the Hudson-Delaware Regions of the Society of Biblical Literature.

5. For a recent discussion of this phenomenon in American culture, see Robert Bellah et al., *Habits of the Heart: Individualism and Commitment in American Life* (New York: Harper & Row, 1985).

6. See Philip E. Slater, *The Pursuit of Loneliness: American Culture at the Breaking Point* (Boston: Beacon Press, 1970), 6-9, Slater discusses the tendency of Americans to seek greater privacy instead of greater interdependence, in the mistaken belief that privacy will supply what they lack in community. A paradox results: "The longing for privacy is generated by the drastic conditions that the longing for privacy produces" (p. 126).

7. Bellah et al., *Habits of the Heart,* 246-47.
8. John T. Pawlikowski, *The Challenge of the Holocaust for Christian Theology* (New York: Anti-Defamation League of B'nai B'rith, 1978), 11.
9. Ibid., 8-9.
10. See *Luther's Works* (American Ed.), vol. 33 (Philadelphia: Fortress Press, 1972).
11. Fresh attention to these metaphors has been paid by Terence E. Fretheim in *The Suffering of God: An Old Testament Perspective* (Philadelphia: Fortress Press, 1984).
12. Joan Didion, *The White Album* (New York: Pocket Books, 1979), 144.
13. Bellah et al., *Habits of the Heart,* 75.
14. Ibid., 77.
15. For further discussion of the categories of story and history in relation to the Bible, see James Barr, *The Scope and Authority of the Bible* (Philadelphia: Westminster Press, 1980), 1-17.
16. Yehuda Bauer, *A History of the Holocaust* (New York: Franklin Watts, 1982), 195.
17. Rubenstein, *Cunning,* p. 49; and Raul Hilberg, *The Destruction of the European Jews* (New York: Harper & Row, 1961), 600-609.
18. Rubenstein, *Cunning,* 67. Emphasis mine.
19. This lack influences the inertia many feel in the face of the nuclear issue. Antiabortion forces and groups fighting gay rights capitalize on this lack as they seek to impose their own programs on society.
20. Geoffrey Vickers, *Freedom in a Rocking Boat: Changing Values in an Unstable Society* (Hammondsworth, Eng.: Penguin Books, 1972), 36-37.
21. Paul D. Hanson, *The Diversity of Scripture: A Theological Interpretation* (Philadelphia: Fortress Press, 1982), 95.

5. God's Presence, Revelation, and Inspiration

1. David Bartlett, *The Shape of Scriptural Authority* (Philadelphia: Fortress Press, 1983).
2. Kelsey, *The Uses of Scripture in Recent Theology* (Philadelphia: Fortress Press, 1975), 9.
3. This incident was described to a class in pastoral counseling by the chaplain involved, the Reverend Lawrence Gudmestad.
4. Daniel J. Boorstin, "Tomorrow: The Republic of Technology," *Time,* January 17, 1977, 37-38.
5. For more extended treatments of this topic, see, e.g., Howard Burkle, *God, Suffering, and Belief* (Nashville: Abingdon Press, 1977), and Douglas John Hall, *God and Human Suffering: An Exercise in the Theology of the Cross* (Minneapolis: Augsburg Pub. House, 1986).
6. For this reason one wishes a personal pronoun more encompassing than he or she were available. The pronoun it is less adequate for God than he, implying an object rather than a person. The pronoun she is as limited as the pronoun he. Combinations such as he/she or himself/herself are overly cumbersome.

7. For another attempt to state the position I explore here, see my "The Role of Words in Revelation," *Word and World* 6 (1986): 278-87.
8. Nor is inspiration, as used here, so broad as to include all great literature. It is limited to that which communicates the revealed presence and identity of God.
9. Hans von Campenhausen, *The Formation of the Christian Bible* (Philadelphia: Fortress Press, 1972), 259.
10. Ibid., 247.
11. Ibid., 205.
12. Irenaeus treasures and makes use of the Apocalypse of John but does not cite it among the normative canonical books; he also cites the Shepherd of Hermas, which is not in our canon. The Muratorian Fragment lists" 'only' two apocalypses, those of John and Peter" (ibid., 219, 247).
13. On target at this point are the objections offered by both J. A. O. Preus, representing a supernaturalist position, and Brevard Childs or James Sanders, representing a supernaturalist position, and Brevard Childs or James Sanders, representing the contemporary school of interpretation known as canon criticism.

6. Biblical Usefulness, Biblical Authority

1. David Kelsey makes a similar point when he says that "part of what it means to call a text 'Christian scripture' is that it decisively shapes persons' identities when it is used in the context of the common life of Christian community" (*The Uses of Scripture in Recent Theology* [Philadelphia: Fortress Press, 1975], 91). Later in his argument (pp. 208-9) he also emphasizes the close tie between the community of faith and the authority of the Scriptures by saying that the doctrine of Scripture finds its proper home with the doctrines of sanctification and ecclesiology.
2. A term borrowed from Michael Polanyi, who employs it in *The Tacit Dimension* (London: Routledge & Kegan Paul, 1966), 4-10. Polanyi notes that "we can know more than we can tell" (p. 4, emphasis omitted). Tacit knowledge enables human beings to recognize what they cannot readily specify or describe. They can, for example, recognize a face without being able to describe it to another person. This awareness is usually gained while attention is on something else: while one is acquiring and attending to specifiable knowledge, one also obtains tacit knowledge. It is this feature that has inspired my adaptation of Polanyi's term. I use the word *tacit* to refer to a development that occurs while people in the community of faith are attending to other tasks—but a development that involves authority rather than, as for Polanyi, knowledge.
3. The discussion that follows has been influenced by insights gleaned from Ernest G. Bormann and Nancy C. Bormann's *Effective Committees and Groups in the Church* (Minneapolis: Augsburg Pub. House, 1973), 47-63. That book does not discuss authority directly but does discuss leadership and how leaders emerge within a small, task-oriented group.
4. Ibid., 13. Emphasis omitted.

5. For an explication of this process, see George Lindbeck, *The Nature of Doctrine: Religion and Theology in a Postliberal Age* (Philadelphia: Westminster Press, 1984), 32-41. My account of the matter seeks to combine the linguistic model Lindbeck favors with an experiential model he criticizes.

6. Antonius H. J. Gunneweg and Walter Schmithals, *Authority*, trans. John E. Steely (Nashville: Abingdon Press, 1982), 18.

7. Richard Sennett, *Authority* (New York: Alfred A. Knopf, 1980) 17-18.

8. Cf. Hans von Campenhausen, *The Formation of the Christian Bible* (Philadelphia: Fortress Press, 1972), 121, 129-30.

9. Under some circumstances the words by which the kerygmatic is proclaimed may need to be adjusted so as to make the message more direct, but the impetus for the adjustment comes from the confessional implications of the proclamation rather than from some internal need. A response that was appropriate in one setting will no longer be appropriate in a different context in which it obscures or distorts the kerygmatic. The Scriptures are full of examples of such adjustments. Some are suggested later in this chapter.

10. The text of the Barmen Declaration can be found in Arthur Cochrane's *The Church's Confession under Hitler* (Philadelphia: Westminster Press, 1962), 237-46.

11. I owe this insight to a public lecture given by Robert Holst at the Institute for Ecumenical and Cultural Research, in 1982.

12. My discussion merely touches on a complex problem. For more information, consult Phyllis Trible, *God and the Rhetoric of Sexuality* (Philadelphia: Fortress Press, 1978), and Elisabeth Schüssler Fiorenza, *In Memory of Her: A Feminist Theological Reconstruction of Christian Origins* (New York: Crossroad, 1983).

13. Cf. Kelsey, *Uses of Scripture*, 7-10, 166, 207.

7. Recontextualizing the Bible

1. Many of the issues discussed in this chapter touch on matters properly included within hermeneutics, which studies the theoretical issues involved in getting a text from one time and place to have meaning for, or speak to a person in, another time and place. I recognize that the philosophical issues are often more complicated than my treatment here indicates.

2. William Countryman, *Biblical Authority or Biblical Tyranny?* (Philadelphia: Fortress Press, 1981), 78-84.

3. I wonder if the difficulty of acknowledging the finitude of our ways does not lie at the bottom of some resistance to historical criticism.

4. George Orwell, *1984* (New York: Harcourt, Brace & Co., 1949).

5. I am using original setting and original context loosely enough to encompass the circumstances under which the words were spoken, preserved in oral form, written down, edited, and canonized. Though I recognize that for any passage the circumstances may have changed as the

words moved from a purely oral expression to canonization in written form, and the change in circumstances may affect the passage's interpretation, the resulting complications do not affect the general principles I outline here. All I affirm is that the meaning of a canonical text can be enhanced by an understanding of its precanonical history.

6. Cf. William Diehl, who recommends that situations be created in which people's experience in their occupations can be taken seriously and brought into dialogue with the Christian faith. "While the local congregation is the appropriate location for the study of the Bible, church history, theology, and the like, it may not be the best place for relating theology and the Bible to complex issues facing people in the workplace. The reason is that the pastor, who has been trained in theology and biblical studies, cannot be expected to have an adequate enough understanding of the complexities of workplace problems to do a credible job of pointing to the how-tos of connecting faith and life" (*In Search of Faithfulness: Lessons from the Christian Community* [Philadelphia: Fortress Press, 1987], 43).

7. Cf. Hanns Lilje, *The Last Book of the Bible: The Meaning of the Revelation of St. John* (Philadelphia: Muhlenberg Press, 1957).

8. Cf. Frederick Buechner, *Telling the Truth: The Gospel as Tragedy, Comedy, and Fairy Tale* (San Francisco: Harper & Row, 1977); idem, *The Magnificent Defeat* (New York: Seabury Press, 1966); idem, *The Hungering Dark* (New York: Seabury Press, 1969); and Richard Jensen, *Telling the Story: Variety and Imagination in Preaching* (Minneapolis: Augsburg Pub. House, 1980). See also my "Story and Scriptures," *Word and World* 1 (1981): 128-39.

Epilogue

1. Augustine, *Confessions* 8.12.

2. For an eloquent plea in behalf of the activities that nurture the faithfulness of Christians and their ministry in daily living, see William Diehl, *In Search of Faithfulness: Lessons from the Christian Community* (Philadelphia: Fortress Press, 1987).

FOR FURTHER READING

Suggested Reading
on Selected Contemporary Themes

Achtemeier, Paul J. *The Inspiration of Scripture: Problems and Proposals.*
Philadelphia: Westminster Press, 1980. Written by a noted biblical scholar for those who already accept the authority of the Bible,
this volume provides a good introduction to the topic of inspiration. Achtemeier weighs carefully strengths and weaknesses
of liberal and conservative views and finds that both depend too
heavily on a prophetic model of inspiration. Achtemeier emphasizes the community of faith and the Spirit's role in the Bible's
effects—sanctifying sinful human beings—instead of its origins.

Barr, James. *Holy Scripture: Canon, Authority, Criticism.* Philadelphia:
Westminster Press, 1983. This series of lectures by a noted Hebrew
Bible scholar, explores the place of biblical research and critical
thinking in the church and its theology. Barr disagrees with Brevard Childs and others who stress the importance of interpreting books of the Bible in terms of their places in the finished canon.
For Barr neither the canonical location of the texts nor their final
form determines correct understanding of the Bible or fosters a
genuinely biblical Christianity. Freedom to explore the written
texts in multiple ways, discerning the persons and lives that stand
behind them, is most important.

———. *The Scope and Authority of the Bible.* Philadelphia: Westminster
Press, 1980. These seven essays discuss the nature, authority, and
use of the Bible. For Barr the Bible is the instrument of faith rather
than its object; biblical authority is built into the structure of
Christianity; it can be freely explored and evaluated, because,
as in a picture, some of its parts are more central than others,
while every part contributes to the whole. Barr argues that the
Bible is better understood as story than as history, and oriented
more to the future than to the past. In the fifth essay he endeavors to understand and assess fundamentalism.

Bartlett, David. *The Shape of Scriptural Authority.* Philadelphia: Fortress
Press, 1983. This brief discussion of authority in the Bible carefully notes the diversity of claims found there. Bartlett locates
four main types: the authority of words, of deeds, of wisdom,
and of witness. (Some interesting parallels exist between these
four types and the four theories discussed in chapters 2 and 3 of

this book: They correspond to the supernaturalist, the ecclesial developmentalist, the analogical developmentalist, and the evangelicalist positions, respectively.

Bellah, Robert, et al. *Habits of the Heart: Individualism and Commitment in American Life*. New York: Harper & Row, 1986 [1985]. This long but important and widely discussed sociological study of American life builds on intensive interviews with a variety of middle-class citizens from different sections of the country. The authors describe an atomistic individualism that they see displacing the republican individualism and biblical individualism of the past. They express concern about the consequences of this for our moral health.

Campenhausen, Hans von. *The Formation of the Christian Bible*. Trans. J. A. Baker. Philadelphia: Fortress Press, 1972. This careful, detailed historical study of the emergence of the canon during the first 200 years of the church's existence explains how and why some Christian writings came to be regarded as religiously authoritative and were gathered into a New Testament. Campenhausen explains how, simultaneously, the church confirmed its acceptance of the Old Testament as holy scripture. Any viable contemporary theory of biblical authority must take into account the theological and practical reasons motivating early Christians to collect and recommend the writings now in our Bible.

Countryman, William. *Biblical Authority or Biblical Tyranny? Scripture and the Christian Pilgrimage*. Philadelphia: Fortress Press, 1981. Written by a New Testament scholar, this book distinguishes (too emphatically, I think) between the absolute authority that belongs to God and the limited authority of the Scriptures. For Countryman the Bible and the church are interdependent; the community of faith exercises a very immediate and practical authority in the lives of most Christians by interpreting the Bible anew for each generation and depending on the Bible to maintain and restore the integrity of its message.

Fretheim, Terence E. *The Suffering of God: An Old Testament Perspective*. Philadelphia: Fortress Press, 1984. This study of biblical metaphors for describing God is a good example of current efforts to rethink the concept of God. Fretheim lays out both the diversity exhibited by these images and the confessional unity that informs them—namely, that the God who saves is always faithful, loving, gracious, and righteous. The presence of God as understood in the Old Testament is discussed in chapter 5 and the suffering of God in chapters 7 through 9.

Jensen, Richard A. *Telling the Story: Variety and Imagination in Preaching*. Minneapolis: Augsburg Pub. House, 1980. Preaching is one of the more important and more public ways in which the Bible is interpreted within the community of faith. Jensen describes didactic preaching, proclamatory preaching, and story preaching, and gives examples of each. Chapter 5, "Story Preaching," is particularly helpful and can be read separately; in it Jensen explains why the story form is currently so attractive, what the story form involves, and how it can be used to interpret the Scriptures.

Kelsey, David. *The Uses of Scripture in Recent Theology*. Philadelphia: Fortress Press, 1975. Kelsey analyzes texts from eight quite different theologians and describes how they actually use the Bible to authenticate their theologies. This descriptive study informs much of what I have to say in this book. However, its abstract language and its primary attention to methodology make it less accessible than most of the others cited here.

Kort, Wesley A. *Story, Text, and Scripture: Literary Interests in Biblical Narrative*. University Park: Pennsylvania State University Press, 1988. This is an introduction to contemporary literary criticism, utilizing the categories of narrative, textuality, and centeredness to construct its own comprehensive view. It calls attention to the importance of the literary form of the Bible. Kort finds plot, character, atmosphere, and tone to be important elements in every narrative–Exodus, Judges, Jonah, and the Gospel of Mark included–and he criticizes each of the four contemporary theories he describes (myth criticism, structural analysis, critical hermeneutics, and composition criticism) because each makes but one of the elements determinative.

Lindbeck, George. *The Nature of Doctrine: Religion and Theology in a Postliberal Age*. Philadelphia: Westminster Press, 1984. While not focusing on the topic of biblical authority or even discussing it directly, this important essay grows out of a conviction that the language of the Bible defines (rather than expresses) the thought-world of the church. Lindbeck, a historical theologian involved in the ecumenical movement, rejects the apologetic approach employed by the theories described here in chapters 2 and 3 in favor of a "cultural-linguistic" approach. He understands the Bible as a narrative story to be entered and understood from the inside. The language of faith is learned by practice and catechesis; doctrines supply the rules of discourse, attitude, and action in the church. As with Kelsey's volume, the approach is abstract and academic, rendering this brief monograph less accessible than most others on this list.

Russell, Letty M., ed. *Feminist Interpretation of the Bible*. Philadelphia: Westminster Press, 1985. Unlike some feminists who feel the Bible must be left behind, the women authors of essays in this book affirm the importance of the Bible and wrestle with its relationship to contemporary women's consciousness. Diverse points of view are expressed, but Russell recommends, in her concluding essay, that within the community of faith a paradigm of "authority as partnership" replace the traditional paradigm of "authority as domination." The essays by Farley, Ruether, and Russell address the topic of contemporary biblical authority most directly.

Vawter, Bruce. *Biblical Inspiration*. Philadelphia: Westminster Press, 1972. A Roman Catholic biblical scholar, this author traces the history of the concept of inspiration from the Bible to the present and offers his own theological assessment. For Vawter inspiration is one aspect in the much larger story of God's communication with human beings and one instance of God's condescension or accommodation to their historical condition. The Bible owes its origin to inspiration and inspiration guides that ongoing interpretation within the community of faith that makes the Bible God's Word.

Wood, Charles M. *The Formation of Christian Understanding: An Essay in Theological Hermeneutics*. Philadelphia: Westminster Press, 1981. A systematic theologian, this author writes a helpful essay on use and interpretation of the Bible as Christian scripture. Wood believes the aim of any Christian interpretation is a deeper knowledge of God; to interpret the Bible with this aim is the same as calling it the Word of God, and this is equivalent to ascribing its authorship to God. For Wood the Bible should be affirmed as canon (regarded as a whole to be the rule for the life and witness of the church) and approached critically (taking the church's contemporary situation into account).

Additional Readings: The Modern Problematic

The Reformation and Post-Reformation Background

Bornkamm, Heinrich. *Luther and the Old Testament*. Trans. Eric W. Gritsch and Ruth C. Gritsch. Philadelphia: Fortress Press, 1969.

Calvin, John. *Institutes of the Christian Religion*. 2 vols. Trans. Ford Lewis Battles; ed. John T. McNeill. Philadelphia: Westminster Press, 1960.

Forstman, Jack. *Word and Spirit: Calvin's Doctrine of Biblical Authority.* Stanford, Calif.: Stanford Univ. Press, 1962.

Hordern, William. *Experience and Faith: The Significance of Luther for Understanding Today's Experiential Religion.* Minneapolis: Augsburg Pub. House, 1983.

Luther, Martin. *Luther's Works.* American ed. 55 vols.; see esp. vol. 35. Ed. Jaroslav Pelikan and Helmut Lehmann. Philadelphia: Fortress Press; St. Louis: Concordia Pub. House, 1955-86.

Oberman, Heiko. *The Harvest of Medieval Theology: Gabriel Biel and Late Medieval Nominalism.* Cambridge: Harvard Univ. Press, 1963.

Preus, James Samuel. *From Shadow to Promise: Old Testament Interpretation from Augustine to the Young Luther.* Cambridge: Harvard Univ. Press, 1969.

Preus, Robert. *The Theology of Post-Reformation Lutheranism.* 2 vols. St. Louis: Concordia Pub. House, 1970-72.

Scharlemann, Robert P. *Thomas Aquinas and John Gerhard.* New Haven: Yale Univ. Press, 1964.

Schmid, Heinrich. *The Doctrinal Theology of the Evangelical Lutheran Church.* Trans. Charles A. Hay and Henry E. Jacobs. Minneapolis: Augsburg Pub. House, 1961 [1889].

Wendel, François. *Calvin: Origins and Development of His Religious Thought.* Trans. Philip Mairet. New York: Harper & Row, 1963.

Theology during the Modern Period

Burtchaell, James T. *Catholic Theories of Biblical Inspiration Since 1810: A Review and Critique.* Cambridge: Cambridge Univ. Press, 1969.

Dayton, Donald W. *Theological Roots of Pentecostalism.* Metuchen, N. J.: Scarecrow Press, 1987.

Forde, Gerhard. *The Law-Gospel Debate: An Interpretation of Its Historical Development.* Minneapolis: Augsburg Pub. House, 1969.

Frei, Hans. *The Eclipse of Biblical Narrative: A Study in Eighteenth and Nineteenth Century Hermeneutics.* New Haven: Yale Univ. Press, 1974.

Hutchison, William R. *The Modernist Impulse in American Protestantism.* New York: Oxford Univ. Press, 1982 [1976].

Jodock, Darrell. "The Impact of Cultural Change: Princeton Theology and Scriptural Authority Today." *Dialog* 22 (1983): 21-29.

Livingston, James C. *Modern Christian Thought: From the Enlightenment to Vatican II.* New York: Macmillan Co., 1971.

Marsden, George M. *Fundamentalism and American Culture: The Shaping of Twentieth-Century Evangelicalism, 1870-1925.* New York: Oxford Univ. Press, 1980.

For Further Reading

Rogers, Jack B., and Donald K. McKim. *The Authority and Interpretation of the Bible: An Historical Approach.* San Francisco: Harper & Row, 1979.
Russell, C. Allyn. *Voices of American Fundamentalism: Seven Biographical Studies.* Philadelphia: Westminster Press, 1976.
Sandeen, Ernest R. *The Roots of Fundamentalism: British and American Millenarianism, 1800-1930.* Grand Rapids: Baker Book House, 1978 [1970].
Welch, Claude, *Protestant Thought in the Nineteenth Century.* Vol. 1, *1799-1870*; vol. 2, *1870-1914*. New Haven: Yale Univ. Press, 1972-85.

Rationalism

Gay, Peter, ed. *Deism: An Anthology.* Princeton: D. Van Nostrand, 1968.
Jefferson, Thomas. *Jefferson's Extracts from the Gospels: The Philosophy of Jesus; and, The Life and Morals of Jesus.* Ed. Dickinson W. Adams. Princeton: Princeton Univ. Press, 1983.
Kant, Immanuel. *Religion within the Limits of Reason Alone.* Trans. Theodore M. Greene and Hoyt H. Hudson. New York: Harper & Bros., 1960 [1934].
Paine, Thomas. *The Age of Reason, Being an Investigation of Time and Fabulous Theology.* Vol. 5, *The Life and Writings of Thomas Paine.* New York: Vincent Parke & Co., 1908.
Reimarus, Hermann Samuel. *Reimarus: Fragments.* Trans. Ralph S. Fraser; ed. Charles H. Talbert. Philadelphia: Fortress Press, 1970.

Supernaturalism

Boice, James Montgomery, ed. *The Foundation of Biblical Authority.* Grand Rapids: Zondervan, 1978.
Hodge, Archibald A., and Benjamin Warfield. *Inspiration.* Grand Rapids: Baker Book House, 1979 [1881].
Machen, J. Gresham. *The Virgin Birth of Christ.* New York: Harper & Bros., 1930.
Preus, J. A. O. "A Statement of Scriptural and Confessional Principles." N. p., n. d. Distributed ca. 1974, while J. A. O. Preus was president of the Lutheran Church-Missouri Synod.
Torrey, R. A., et al. *The Fundamentals: A Testimony to the Truth.* 4 vols. Grand Rapids: Baker Book House, 1980 [1917].
Warfield, Benjamin Breckinridge. *The Works of Benjamin Warfield.* 10 vols. Grand Rapids: Baker Book House, 1981 [1927-32].

Evangelicalism

Dreyer, Frederick. "Faith and Experience in the Thought of John Wesley." *American Historical Review* 88 (1983): 12-30.

Finney, Charles Grandison. *Lectures on Revivals of Religion.* Cambridge: Harvard Univ. Press, 1960. (Especially Lecture IX, "Means to be Used with Sinners.")
Outler, Albert, ed. *John Wesley.* New York: Oxford Univ. Press, 1964.
Shelton, Larry. "John Wesley's Approach to Scripture in Historical Perspective." *Wesleyan Theological Journal* 16 (1981): 23-50.

Ecclesial Developmentalism

Hodgson, Peter C. *The Formation of Historical Theology: A Study of Ferdinand Christian Baur.* New York: Harper & Row, 1966.
Schleiermacher, Friedrich. *Brief Outline on the Study of Theology.* Trans. Terrence Tice. Richmond: John Knox Press, 1966.
————. *The Christian Faith.* Trans. H. R. Mackintosh and J. S. Stewart. Edinburgh: T. & T. Clark, 1928.
————. *On Religion: Speeches to Its Cultured Despisers.* Trans. John Oman. New York: Harper & Bros., 1958 [1893].

Analogical Developmentalism

Beardslee, William A. *A House for Hope: A Study in Process and Biblical Thought.* Philadelphia: Westminster Press, 1972.
Cargas, Harry James, and Bernard Lee, eds. *Religious Experience and Process Theology: The Pastoral Implications of a Major Modern Movement.* New York: Paulist Press, 1976.
Griffin, David R. "Relativism, Divine Causation, and Biblical Theology." *Encounter* 36 (1975): 342-60.
Hegel, Georg Wilhelm Friedrich. *Lectures on the Philosophy of Religion.* 3 vols. Trans. R. F. Brown, P. C. Hodgson, and J. M. Stewart; ed. P. C. Hodgson. Berkeley and Los Angeles: Univ. of California Press, 1984-87.
Whitehead, Alfred North. *Religion in the Making.* New York: Macmillan Co., 1926.

Dynamic Humanism

Feuerbach, Ludwig. *The Essence of Christianity.* Trans. George Eliot. New York: Harper & Bros., 1956 [1854].
————. *Lectures on the Essence of Religion.* Trans. Ralph Manheim. New York: Harper & Row, 1967.
Strauss, David Friedrich. *The Life of Jesus Critically Examined.* Trans. George Eliot; ed. Peter C. Hodgson. Philadelphia: Fortress Press, 1972.

Additional Readings: The Postmodern Problematic

Contemporary Culture

Didion, Joan. *The White Album*. New York: Pocket Books, 1979.

Orwell, George. *1984*. New York: Harcourt, Brace & Co., 1949.

Slater, Philip E. *The Pursuit of Loneliness: American Culture at the Breaking Point*. Boston: Beacon Press, 1970.

Vickers, Geoffrey. *Freedom in a Rocking Boat: Changing Values in an Unstable Society*. Hammondsworth, Eng.: Penguin Books, 1972 [1970].

Theological Reflections

Baillie, John. *The Sense of the Presence of God*. New York: Charles Scribner's Sons, 1962.

Boer, Harry R. *The Bible and Higher Criticism*. Grand Rapids: Wm. B. Eerdmans, 1981. Originally published in 1975 under the title *Above the Battle? The Bible and Its Critics*.

Childs, Brevard S. *Introduction to the Old Testament as Scripture*. Philadelphia: Fortress Press, 1979.

Diehl, William. *In Search of Faithfulness: Lessons from the Christian Community*. Philadelphia: Fortress Press, 1987.

Dodd, C. H. *The Authority of the Bible*. Rev. ed. London: William Collins Sons, 1960.

Farley, Edward. *Ecclesial Reflection: An Anatomy of Theological Method*. Philadelphia: Fortress Press, 1982.

Frei, Hans. *The Identity of Jesus Christ: The Hermeneutical Bases of Dogmatic Theology*. Philadelphia: Fortress Press, 1975.

Gnuse, Robert. *The Authority of the Bible: Theories of Inspiration, Revelation, and the Canon of Scripture*. New York: Paulist Press, 1985.

Greenspahn, Frederick, ed. *Scripture in the Jewish and Christian Traditions: Authority, Interpretation, Relevance*. Nashville: Abingdon Press, 1982.

Hanson, Paul D. *The Diversity of Scripture: A Theological Interpretation*. Philadelphia: Fortress Press, 1982.

McKim, Donald K. *What Christians Believe about the Bible*. Nashville: Thomas Nelson, 1985.

Nineham, David. *The Use and Abuse of the Bible: A Study of the Bible in an Age of Rapid Cultural Change*. New York: Barnes & Noble, 1976.

Schüssler-Fiorenza, Elisabeth. *Bread not Stone: The Challenge of Feminist Biblical Interpretation*, Boston: Beacon Press, 1984.

———. *In Memory of Her: A Feminist Theological Reconstruction of Christian Origins*. New York: Crossroad, 1983.

Thiemann, Ronald F. *Revelation and Theology: The Gospel as Narrated Promise*. Notre Dame: Univ. of Notre Dame Press, 1985.
Trible, Phyllis. *God and the Rhetoric of Sexuality*. Philadelphia: Fortress Press, 1978.
Wink, Walter. *The Bible in Human Transformation: Toward a New Paradigm for Biblical Study*. Philadelphia: Fortress Press, 1973.

Authority

Bormann, Ernest G., and Nancy C. Bormann. *Effective Committees and Groups in the Church*. Minneapolis: Augsburg Pub. House, 1973.
Gunneweg, Antonius H. J., and Walter Schmithals. *Authority*. Trans. John E. Steely. Nashville: Abingdon Press, 1982.
Sennett, Richard. *Authority*. New York: Alfred A. Knopf, 1980.

Narrative

Buechner, Frederick. *The Hungering Dark*. New York: Seabury Press, 1969.
———. *The Magnificent Defeat*. New York: Seabury Press, 1966.
———. *Telling the Truth: The Gospel as Tragedy, Comedy, and Fairy Tale*. San Francisco: Harper & Row, 1977.
Jodock, Darrell. "Story and Scriptures." *Word and World* 1 (1981): 128-39.
Stroup, George W. *The Promise of Narrative Theology: Recovering the Gospel in the Church*. Atlanta: John Knox Press, 1981.

The Holocaust, God, and Suffering

Bauer, Yehuda. *A History of the Holocaust*. New York: Franklin Watts, 1982.
Burkle, Howard R. *God, Suffering, and Belief*. Nashville: Abingdon Press, 1977.
Cochrane, Arthur C. *The Church's Confession under Hitler*. Philadelphia: Westminster Press, 1962.
Hall, Douglas John. *God and Human Suffering: An Exercise in the Theology of the Cross*. Minneapolis: Augsburg Pub. House, 1986.
Hilberg, Raul. *The Destruction of the European Jews*. New York: Harper & Row, 1961.
Pawlikowski, John T. *The Challenge of the Holocaust for Christian Theology*. New York: Anti-Defamation League of B'nai B'rith, 1978.
Rubenstein, Richard L. *The Cunning of History: Mass Death and the American Future*. New York: Harper & Row, 1975.

Index

Aaron, 49, 58
Abélard, 20
Abraham, 94, 115, 123
Absence (of God), 95-96
Acts of the Apostles, 100, 123-24
Amish, Old Order, 25
Analogical developmentalism, 31, 51-
53, 58-67, 71, 127, 152, 153
Anselm of Canterbury, 27, 149
Apocalyptic writings, 101, 142, 156
Apostolic, 99-101, 112, 142
Archaeology, 44
Aristotle, 21
Augustine (of Hippo), 145, 158
Auschwitz, 8, 82
Authoritarianism, 10, 85
Authority, church, 1, 2, 20-21, 47
cultural, 8, 9-10, 86
the nature of, 11, 33-34, 74, 88, 105-
12, 115-16, 117-18, 119, 120
Autonomous reason (as value in
modern culture), 16, 26-28, 40, 47,
56, 60-61, 63
Awe, 117-18

Baptist, 50
Barmen Declaration, 121, 157
Barr, J., 155
Bartlett, D., 89, 155
Bauer, Y., 155
Baur, F. C., 151, 153
Beardslee, W., 60, 153
Bellah, R., 154, 155
Bellamy, E., 154
Biel, G., 148
Boorstin, D., 96, 155
Bormann, E. and N., 156
Buechner, F., 158
Bultmann, R., 152
Burkle, H., 155

Call (divine), 11, 49, 115, 119, 142-43,
145

Calov, A., 28
Calvin, J., 134
Calvinist, 22, 23, 45
Campenhausen, H. von, 101, 148, 156,
157
Canon, 7, 23, 101, 112-13, 134, 141, 156
Caven, W., 151
Childs, B., 7, 147, 156
Christendom, 9, 24, 25, 27, 87
Church, 4, 11, 20, 22, 42, 48, 55, 57,
62, 75-76, 113, 114, 115, 124, 125,
132, 137-38
Civil religion, 96, 136
Classical theism, 23, 78, 87, 127-28
Community, 19, 56, 62, 63, 73, 74, 75,
94, 105-7, 110, 132, 154
Community of faith (Christian com-
munity), 5, 10, 11, 19, 29, 53, 55,
56, 61, 66, 74, 75, 76, 80, 83, 84,
86, 91, 100, 101, 103, 106-8, 109,
110-11, 115-17, 117-18, 122, 123,
125, 127, 129, 132, 137-145, 156
Communication of God's presence,
99-100, 101, 103, 107, 112, 116-17,
125, 139-40
Confessional nature of the Bible, 120-
25, 128, 138
Conservative(s), 25, 28, 37-38, 49-50,
52, 64, 84, 85, 108, 141, 149
Context, 8, 32, 57, 66, 67, 71, 83, 90-
91, 95, 102, 105-6, 108, 119-20,
122, 124-25, 129-32, 133-35, 140,
157, 158
Continuity (in the church), 118-19, 124
Corinthians, first Epistle to, 75, 99,
115, 124, 137
second Epistle to, 99
Countryman, W., 157
Creeds, 17
Culture Protestantism, 9

Darwin, C., 52, 72

169

David (King), 123, 136
Deductive arguments (for biblical authority), 44-45
Deism, 16, 128, 150
Depression, the Great, 9
Designated authority, 111, 113
Detachment of self, 17-18
Deuteronomy, Book of, 120-21
Developmentalist understanding of the past, 28, 33, 34, 38, 51, 52, 53-58, 59-62, 64-67, 149
Didion, J., 79-80, 155
Diehl, W., 158
Diversity, cultural, 72, 82, 126
  in the church, 115, 126, 137-38, 142
  in the Scriptures, 57, 89, 114, 120, 121, 124, 134, 136-38
Doctrine, 17, 27-28, 41, 44, 45, 47-49, 52, 57, 62, 118, 139, 150, 153
Dynamic humanism, 31, 62-65, 149, 150, 154

Ecclesial developmentalism, 31, 51-58, 59, 62, 63-64, 65-67, 71, 127, 153
Ecumenical, 1, 5-7, 137
Einstein, A., 72
Engaged use (of the Bible), 5, 10, 11, 87
Enlightenment, the, 15, 36
Evangelicalism, 31, 46-53, 55, 57, 58, 64, 65-67, 71, 117, 127, 152
Exodus, the, 29, 39, 45, 49, 55, 58, 62, 64, 122, 136
Exodus, Book of, 39, 94, 122
Experience, 46, 49, 50, 59, 71, 93-95, 97, 99, 107, 116-17, 118, 127, 152, 154, 158
Extrabiblical considerations (in biblical authority), 32, 34, 50, 65-67, 71, 76, 90, 105, 126
Ezekiel, 143

Faith, 16, 17, 21, 28, 49, 55, 57, 67, 86, 117, 130, 145, 154, 158
Feuerbach, L., 154
Film, 73

Fiorenza, E. Schüssler, 157
Freedom, 1, 8, 35, 36, 39, 58, 64, 77, 80, 87, 121, 150
French Revolution, 26
Fretheim, T., 155
Freud, S., 73
Functional authority, 105-14
Fundamentalism, fundamentalists, 25, 114, 148

Genesis, Book of, 19, 45, 65, 80, 84, 133, 134, 135, 148
Gerstner, J., 44, 151
Gnosticism, 141
God, concept of, 4, 5, 9, 11, 23, 32, 33, 59-60, 65-66, 78, 86, 87, 90-93, 98
Gospel, 10, 22, 66-67, 84, 86, 90, 99
Gospels, the, 37, 44, 150
Grace of God, 29, 36, 40, 46, 57, 93, 100, 120, 121, 143
Gray, J., 151
Griffin, D., 58, 153
Gunneweg, A., 117, 157

Hall, D. J., 155
Hanson, P., 85, 155
Harnack, A. von, 147-48
Hartshorne, C., 153
Hegel, G., 58, 59, 153
Heisenberg, W., 72
Hengstenberg, E., 151
Hermeneutics, 157
Historical criticism, 2, 6-8, 38, 50, 53, 60, 101-2, 103, 129-30, 131, 141, 148, 150, 157
Historical distance, 7, 86, 129-30, 143, 147
History, 4, 28, 29, 42-43, 50, 54, 57, 65, 66, 80, 131, 153, 154, 155
Hofmann, J. C. K. von, 152
Holocaust, 72-73, 77, 81-82, 88, 106, 121-22, 134
Holy Spirit, 46, 48, 55, 56, 100, 101, 110, 123, 141, 142, 143, 152
Holst, R., 157
Homosexuality, ix, 89, 138

Index

Human potential (as value in modern culture), 18, 36, 41, 47, 57, 61, 63
Humanism, 54, 62-65, 147

Identity, human, 80, 88, 93-94, 100, 101, 103, 107, 138-139
of God, 4, 78, 80, 83, 84, 88, 92, 99, 100, 101, 103, 122, 125, 127, 138, 139, 142, 156
Imagination, 86, 130, 139-40
Immanence, 4, 57
Incarnation, 51, 59
Individualism, 8, 9, 18-19, 28-29, 36, 41, 48-49, 56, 61, 63, 73, 75, 76, 84, 88
Inductive arguments (for biblical authority), 43-44
Industrial Revolution, 15, 36
Inerrancy, of the Bible, 102-3
Infallibility, of the Bible, 102-3, 149
Inspiration, 2, 5, 23, 44, 52, 67, 89-90, 100-2, 103, 110, 143, 148, 150, 156
Integrated view of the Bible, 2-3, 4, 6, 8, 9
Integrity, 10, 135-37
Interdependence, 87-88, 98
Involvement of self, 18
Irenaeus, 101, 112-13, 156
Isaiah, 48
Islam, 17, 24
Isolation, personal, 96
Israel/ Israelites, 39, 44, 46, 49, 58, 62, 66, 92, 93, 94, 121, 123, 133, 135, 136

Jefferson, T., 37, 150
Jensen, R., 158
Jeremiah, 94, 141
Book of, 121
Jesus the Christ, 4, 28, 29, 36, 37, 51, 54, 55, 56, 58, 59, 74, 84, 100, 109, 118, 119, 122, 124, 125, 126, 142, 152, 153
John, first Epistle of, 107, 121
Gospel of, 107, 121, 123, 124

Judaism, 17, 19, 24, 84
Justification, 6

Kant, I., 150
Kelsey, D., 90, 92, 149, 155, 156, 157
Kerygmatic (nature of the Bible), 120-21, 122-25, 128, 138, 157
Kingdom of God, 85, 87, 140
Kyle, M. G., 44, 151

Language of faith, 114, 116-18, 119, 123, 125, 126
Law and gospel, 22
Liberals, liberal or critical view of the Bible, 25, 28, 52, 84, 86, 108, 141
Lilje, H., 134, 158
Lindbeck, G., 157
Literal view of the Bible, 64
Loisy, A., 6, 152
Loneliness, 75-76, 96
Luke, Gospel of, 113, 121, 123, 124, 142
Luther, M., 21, 22, 78, 97, 134
Lutheran, 22, 23, 45, 50

Machen, J.G., 42-43, 150, 151
Marcion, 112-13
Mark, Gospel of, 107, 121, 142
Marty, M., 149
Marx, K., 73, 149, 154
Matthew, Gospel of, 6, 75, 112
Mechanical view of the universe, 19, 29, 35, 40, 46, 57, 61-62, 63-64, 65, 96
Mennonites, 83
Methodist, 50, 131
Middle Ages, 1, 16, 17, 20, 21, 123, 147
Miracle(s), 1, 34, 35, 38, 39-40, 42-45, 48, 49, 54, 58, 62, 65, 78, 97-98, 152
Modern culture, 1, 3, 8, 10, 15-19, 24-29, 31, 32, 34, 39, 41-43, 46, 50-53, 55-57, 60-61, 65, 67, 71, 74, 96, 124, 127, 131, 147, 152, 153
definition of, 15-19

171

Modernism, 25, 52
  Roman Catholic, 5-6
Montanism, 101, 123, 141-42
Moral law, 36, 39, 72
Moses, 46, 49, 58, 94, 152

Nathan, the prophet, 136
Nationalism, 26
Natural law, 36, 38, 39, 40, 64, 72
Neo-orthodoxy, 8, 9
Neo-pietism, 152
New religious right, 9
New Testament, 43, 52, 60-84, 101,
  112-13, 118, 121, 123, 141
Nineham, D., 150
Nominalism, 21
Nuclear arms/power, 72, 77, 89, 125

Oberman, H., 148
Objectivity (as value in modern cul-
  ture), 17-18, 28, 40-41, 47, 56, 61,
  63, 72, 96
Old Testament, 43, 60, 84, 113, 118
Ontological argument, 27
Optimism, 8, 18, 28, 36, 41, 47, 56, 57,
  61, 63, 72, 97
Ordination of women, 6, 124
Orthodox, Eastern, 5
Orwell, G., 130, 157

Patriarchs, 33, 55
Paine, T., 149
Paul, the apostle, 6, 48, 75, 99, 102, 107,
  113, 115, 121, 122-24, 137, 138
Pawlikowski, J., 77, 155
Pelikan, J., 74, 154
Pentateuch, 102, 121, 123, 152
Pentecost, 100, 115
Pius X, 6, 151, 153
Plato, 21
Polanyi, M., 156
Postmodern culture, 2, 3, 8-10, 71-74,
  76-77, 79-88, 95-96, 126, 153
Post-Reformation period, 22, 24

Post-Reformation theology, 22-23, 26,
  27, 28, 31, 41-42, 45, 48, 50, 51,
  57, 62, 71, 78, 148
Power of God, 87-88, 94-95, 98
Praxis, 18, 87, 108
Predestination, 95
Premillennialism, 25
Premodern culture, 15, 20-24, 27, 34,
  45
Presbyterian, 50
Presence, 93
  of God, 87-88, 89, 93-103, 107, 114-
  15, 116, 117-120, 125, 127, 134,
  137, 142, 143, 156
Preus, J.A.O., 151, 156
Preus, R., 148, 149
Process philosophy, 58
Prophecy, 43-44
Prophets, 29, 55, 122
Progress (as value in modern cul-
  ture), 1, 16-17, 27-28, 36, 40, 47,
  56, 61, 63, 72, 96
Protestants, 5, 6, 9, 20, 22, 23, 31, 148
Protestant America, 9
Puritans, 136

Rationalism, 31, 34-39, 40, 45, 46, 52,
  54, 56-58, 60-61, 63, 64, 128, 151,
  152
Reason, 16, 20, 21, 27, 36, 37, 41, 46,
  49, 50, 60-61, 63, 73, 150
Recontextualizing (Scripture), 129-43,
  145
Reformation, Protestant, 1, 20, 21-22,
  78, 95
Reformed. *See* Calvinist.
Reimarus, 149-50
Relativism, 9, 82, 84, 85, 96
Renaissance, 20, 22
Renan, E., 149
Reumann, J., 147
Revelation, 2, 4, 9, 21, 28, 40, 41, 49,
  54, 56, 57, 67, 89-90, 93-103, 114-
  15, 118-20, 122-26, 142
Revelation, Book of, 45, 64, 80, 84, 134,
  142, 156, 158

Ricoeur, P., 7, 147
Ritschl, A., 152, 153
Rituals, 11, 18, 36
Roman Catholic(s), 5, 6, 20-23, 45, 50
Roman Empire, 16, 19
Romans, Epistle to, 27, 122
Rubenstein, R., 72, 81-82, 154, 155

Samuel, 48
Sandeen, E., 148
Sanders, James, 156
Scharlemann, R., 148
Schleiermacher, F., 152, 153
Schmid, H., 148
Schmithals, W., 117, 157
Scholasticism (Medieval), 20, 22
Schoolmen, 20
Science, natural, 17
"Scripture alone," 6, 21, 22
Scripture and tradition, 6, 22
Sennett, R., 117, 157
Septuagint, 113, 119
Service (Christian), 11, 19
Shalom, 80, 88, 143
Sin, 4, 18, 40, 47, 56, 95, 110
Slater, P., 154
Slavery, 1, 123, 125
Static understanding of the past, 28, 33, 34, 38, 39, 42, 45, 46, 49, 50, 54, 64-66
Story, 62, 79-81, 85, 86, 88, 138-39, 142, 155
Strauss, D., 149, 150, 151
Suffering, 60, 96-97
Supernaturalism, 31, 39-46, 48-55, 57-58, 64-67, 71, 102, 127, 151, 156
Symbolic view of the Bible, 64
Symbols, 18, 36, 61, 62, 63, 86

Television, 15, 73, 96
Theory of biblical authority, importance of, 5, 10-11, 76
Thomas Aquinas, 20
Tiede, D., ix
Timothy, second Epistle to, 105
Tindal, M., 149

Toland, J., 149
Torah, 29
Tradition, 17, 18, 23, 28, 47, 60, 61, 65
Tradition, church, 6, 20, 21, 23, 25, 31, 37
Transcendence, 4, 63, 76-78, 85, 96, 118, 142
Transparency, in language, 78, 80, 88, 100, 102-3, 114, 121, 139
Trible, P., 157
Trinity, 1, 148
Triumphalism, 10
Truth, 10, 40, 41, 46, 56, 59, 60-62, 143

Use of the Bible, 10, 74, 107, 112, 113, 114, 118, 145

Values, 17, 80-83, 85, 86
Vatican Council II, 6
Vawter, B., 148
Vickers, G., 82, 155
Vietnam War, 8
Virgin birth, 42-43
Voltaire, 149, 150

Warfield, B., 150, 151
Wesley, J., 131, 152
Wesleyan, 50
Whitehead, A. N., 59, 153
Wink, W., 7, 147
Women, status of, ix, 6, 85, 89, 123-24
Word of God, 22, 23, 45, 99, 120, 141, 143
World War I, 8, 72
Worship, 11, 19, 36, 47, 112, 115, 118, 120
Wright, G. E., 151

Yeats, W. B., 154

Zwinglian, 45